Saints
with a difference

J. P. Vaswani

Sterling Paperbacks

Books and Booklets By J.P. Vaswani

In English:

The Seven Commandments of the Bhagavad Gita
Kill Fear Before Fear Kills You
Swallow Irritation Before Irritation Swallows You
Its All A Matter of Attitude
You Can Make A Difference
101 Stories For You and Me
108 Pearls of Practical Wisdom
108 Simple Prayers of A Simple Man
108 Thoughts on Success
114 Thoughts on Love
A Child of God
A Day with Dadaji
A Mystic of Modern India
Begin the Day with God
Beloved Dadaji
Conversations with Dadaji
Dada Answers
Daily Appointment With God
Daily Inspiration
Doors of Heaven
Education: What India Needs
Feast of Love
Five Fragrant Flowers
From Darkness Into Light
From Hell to Heaven
Glimpses
Glimpses Into Great Lives
God In Quest of Man
Hinduism
How to Have Real Fun Out of Life and other Talks
How to Make Your Life A Love Story
How to Overcome Temptations
How to Overcome Tensions
I Have Need of You
I Luv U, God!
Invest in the Child
Joy Peace Pills
Laugh Your Way to Health
Life After Death
Life is A Love Story
Love and Laugh!
Nestle Now
Notes from the Master's Lute
Pictures and Parables
Positive Power of Thanksgiving
Prayers of A Pilgrim
Prophets and Patriots
Sadhu Vaswani: His Life and Teachings
Little Lamps
Secrets of Health and Happiness
Shanti Speaks
Snacks for the Soul
More Snacks for the Soul
Stories for Meditation
Stories for You and Me
Teach Me to Pray
Tear-Drops (poems)

Temple Flowers
Ten Commandents of A Successful Marriage
The Holy Man of Hyderabad
The Kingdom of Krishna
A Little Book of Life
A Little Book of Wisdom
The Little Book of Prayer
The Little Book of Service
The Little Book of Success
The Little Book of Yoga
The Little Book of Freedom From Stress
The Magic of Forgiveness
The Simple Way
The Story of A Simple Man
The Way of *Abhyasa* (How to Meditate)
Ticket to Heaven
Twinkle, Twinkle Tiny Star
What You Would Like to Know about *Karma*
Whispers
Why Do Good People Suffer?
You Are Not Alone!
You Can Be A Smile Millionaire
Destination Happiness
Ladder of *Abhyasa*
Peace or Perish – There is no Other Choice
Good Parenting
Teachers Are Sculptors
I am a Sindhi
The Perfect Relationship: Guru and Disciple

Sketches of Saints Known & Unknown
Short Sketches of Saints Known & Unknown
Management: Moment by Moment
Thus Have I Been Taught
Dewdrops of Love
A Treasure of Quotes
Living Legend
Saints for You and Me
Does God Have Favourites?
Nearer, My God, to Thee!
90 Vegetarian Sindhi Recipes
Many Paths: One Goal

In Hindi:

Ishwar Tujhe Pranaam
Prarthna Ki Shakti
Alwar Santon Ki Mahaan Gaathaayein
Atmik Jalpaan
Atmik Poshan
Bhale Logon Ke Saath Bura Kyon
Chitra Darshan
Dainik Prerna
Krodh Ko Jalayen, Swayam Ko Nahi
Mahan Purush Jeevan Darshan
Santon Ki Lila
Mrityun Hai Dwaar : Phir Kya?
Safal Vivah Ke Dus Rahasya
Jiski Jholi Main Hai Pyaar
Dar Se Mukti
Laghu Kathayein

Published by
Sterling Publishers Private Limited

STERLING PAPERBACKS
An imprint of
Sterling Publishers (P) Ltd.
A-59, Okhla Industrial Area, Phase-II, New Delhi-110020.
Tel: 26387070, 26386209; Fax: 91-11-26383788
E-mail: mail@sterlingpublishers.com
ghai@nde.vsnl.net.in
www.sterlingpublishers.com

Saints with a difference
© 2010, J. P. Vaswani
ISBN 978 81 207 4961 0

All rights are reserved.
No part of this publication may be reproduced, stored in a retrieval system or transmitted, in any form or by any means, mechanical, photocopying, recording or otherwise, without prior written permission of the author.

DADA VASWANI BOOKS
Visit us online to purchase books on self improvement, spiritual advancement, meditation and philosophy. Plus audio cassettes, CDs, DVDs, monthly journals and books in Hindi.
www.dadavaswanisbooks.org

Printed in India
Printed and Published by Sterling Publishers Pvt. Ltd., New Delhi-110 020.

Contents

Ambapali 1
Karaikkal Ammaiyar 18
Sri Vallabhacharya 34
Guru Tegh Bahadur 46
Janabai 64
Sri Annamacharya 79
Bilwa Mangal 89
Guru Amar Das 105
Mira 117
Keshub Chandra Sen 131
Kanakadasa 142
Maharishi Narada 150
St. Monica 175
The Unknown Baba 189
Martin Luther King Jr. 200
Chandana 214
Milarepa 227

Sage Veda Vyasa 248
Moses 261
Jhoolelal 274

Ambapali

Ambapali was one of those great souls whose life is a standing proof of the fact that enlightenment and liberation are open to all human beings who aspire for self-realisation. She turned her back upon a life of wealth and comfort to offer all she was, and all she had, at the lotus-feet of the Buddha. The Master too, saw beyond external appearances to understand her spiritual aspirations, and accepted her into his fold, to follow the path of dhamma.

Ambapali

Ambapali, also known as Amrapali or Ambapalika, was one of those chosen, fortunate souls whose life was transformed through direct, personal contact with Gautama, the Buddha. How did this transformation come to pass? How was the Royal Courtesan of the kingdom of Vaishali elevated to the status of discipleship of the great Master? Her fascinating story has come down to us through Buddhist scriptures as well as popular legends, for it was a story that captured the imagination of the people.

When he became the Enlightened One, the Buddha chose to share his wisdom with the people. He was not one of those teachers with a 'closed fist' who kept back special knowledge from their disciples. When he was blessed with the ultimate knowledge of the truth of life, he said to himself, "This knowledge is not only for me. This knowledge is to be shared with the grief-stricken world. I will travel from place to place to impart this knowledge to the people, and show them the path, treading which they may achieve liberation."

In the caste-ridden, divided society of the times, the Buddha did not discriminate between rich and poor, high and low born people. Men and women, young and old, rich and poor, princes and paupers came to listen to his wise words, and he received everyone with love and courtesy and gladly shared his wisdom with one and all. Thus, the Buddha kept travelling and preaching for many years. When he turned 80 years old, he said to himself, "Now I must start preparing myself to leave this world to proceed on my heavenly journey." He had difficulty in walking due to old age, but went to Magadh, which was a place dear to him. Then he crossed the river Ganga and went towards the north.

When he and his followers reached the city of Vaishali, they were invited to stay in the mango orchard belonging to one of the most famous citizens of Vaishali – the beautiful courtesan named Ambapali.

Who was Ambapali and why was she named thus? Although ancient history books do not tell us much about women, this lady was accepted as one of the Buddha's disciples and her story is mentioned in many of the ancient Buddhist scriptures. Her name is derived from two Sanskrit words; *amba* (mango) and *pali* (tender leaves or shoots). She was of unknown parentage. It is said that as a baby, she was found under a mango tree in one of Vaishali's royal orchards, and was bestowed with this name. She grew up to be a lady of extraordinary beauty, charm and grace – "as lovely as the golden sun rising from the ocean," according to a

Pali text. She was thought to be the most beautiful girl on this earth. Every eligible young man in Vaishali aspired to offer his hand in marriage to her; in fact kings and princes from neighbouring provinces also wanted to marry her. There was just one Ambapali, but the aspirants to her hand were many!

In order to avoid bitter rivalry and strife among these powerful men, Ambapali was proclaimed to be the state Courtesan of Vaishali. After all, they reasoned, she had been brought up as the daughter of a dancer, and could therefore be forced to live a 'public' life, as the consort of many men, instead of being the wife of one man. Ambapali was thus forced to become a courtesan – a woman subservient to many 'patrons'. She was forced into a life of immorality; but in the process, she became very rich. People started saying that Ambapali was not only the most beautiful, but also the wealthiest woman in the town. She owned many palaces and plenty of land, orchards and groves.

Legends record that King Bimbisara of Magadh, heard of her beauty and decided to attack Vaishali in order to gain access to her. It is said that he was entertained as a guest by Ambapali in her palace, and actually agreed to withdraw his attack on Vaishali, due to her persuasions. This made her even more popular in the eyes of the people.

When the Buddha reached Vaishali, he rested for a while in the cool shade of a grove of mango trees on the outskirts of the town. It was one of Ambapali's orchards, and when she heard about the Buddha's arrival, she sent a messenger inviting him to use her orchard as his resting place while he was in Vaishali. The Buddha graciously accepted her offer, and camped there with his followers. The people of Vaishali came in great numbers to see him and listen to his sacred discourses.

All this while, Ambapali chose not to go in person to meet the Buddha, for she felt that she was unworthy of having his *darshan*. However, one of her ladies-in-waiting, decided to attend the daily discourses being held at her mistress's grove, and to catch a glimpse of the great Master about whom everyone had something good to say. As she mingled with the crowd, she heard the Buddha address his followers thus: "Let a brother, O *bhikkhus*, be mindful and thoughtful. Let a brother, whilst in the world, overcome the grief which arises from bodily craving, from the lust of sensations, and from the errors of wrong reasoning. Whatever you do, act always in full presence of mind, in full awareness. Be thoughtful, be aware, in eating and drinking, in walking or standing, in sleeping or waking, while talking or being silent."

The servant was so impressed with what she saw and heard, that she decided to report it all to her mistress.

The moment of spiritual awakening which comes only to the chosen few, was close at hand for Ambapali. She had been feeling restless and ill at ease for sometime; a great conflict had been raging in her mind; she was unable to rest peacefully. All the wealth, the palaces, lands and property that she owned gave her no security or comfort now. "I have everything I need, and all that I could want," she thought to herself, "and yet I don't know why my mind is disturbed and not at peace. What should I do?"

One of her friends said to her, "Ambapali, you are much better off than married women in our society. You enjoy the kind of freedom and power which they can never hope to have from their husbands."

But Ambapali said to her, "This freedom disturbs me. I am in search of another kind of freedom, but I do not know where I can find it. Who will give me that freedom?"

It was then that her servant came to tell her of the Buddha. "Lady, please permit me to tell you what I have seen and heard. All the nobles and princes as well as the common people of Vaishali went on foot to our grove of mangoes yesterday. When I asked them why they had gone there, they said that it was because of the man who is resting there. They say that there are no others like him. He is the son of a king and has given up his kingdom so that he might find the Truth. I had the privilege of seeing him and listening to him today. Truly, I feel blessed. I desire that you too, may be blessed by his *darshan*."

Ambapali's heart was touched when she heard about the Buddha. She thought to herself, "May be this Mahatma could give me the answer to the queries that have been troubling me. May be he can show me the way to the truth I am seeking." Straightaway, she ordered her carriage to be brought. Discarding her expensive silken robes and gold jewels, she donned a simple dress and took the carriage to her mango orchard. As she approached the grove, she found the way jammed with milling crowds who were struggling to get in through the entrance. Ordering her carriage to stop, she walked all the way to reach her grove, and sought to find the Buddha. It was very quiet inside the orchard; even the leaves did not stir. Lady Ambapali walked quietly through the garden, until she saw beneath the deep shade of tall trees a man who could only have been the Buddha, seated with folded hands and feet. Around his head an aura glowed like the midnight moon.

God had gifted Ambapali with wondrous beauty: rarely had anyone on this earth been gifted with such good looks! But at this moment, she lost all consciousness of her self; she stood there amazed, forgetting her beauty, forgetting herself, forgetting all but the Blessed One. Right there, her whole heart melted and flowed away in a river of tears. Very slowly, she approached the Buddha and fell before his feet, laying her face on the earth.

This is what the ancient Buddhist texts tell us of this rare encounter between the beautiful courtesan and the Enlightened One:

The Blessed One thought to himself, "This woman moves in worldly circles and is a favourite of kings and princes; yet is her heart calm and composed. Young in years, rich, surrounded by pleasures, she is thoughtful and steadfast. This, indeed, is rare in the world. Although living in luxury, she has acquired the wisdom of a master, taking delight in piety, and is able to receive the truth in its completeness."

The Buddha asked her to rise and take her seat in the congregation. She gently sat at his holy feet and said to him, "I have everything that this world can give, wealth and possessions, name and fame, all the worldly pleasures, but what do I do about the sad plight of my mind? I feel just like a weather-beaten boat that has got sucked into a terrible whirlpool of water and is being dragged under the overwhelming floods. Try as much as I can, I am unable to extricate myself from this whirlpool. This is the state of my mind. I have spent many years in leading the life of a courtesan, and now my slumbering soul has awakened. Is there any hope for me?"

The Buddha replied compassionately, "For everyone the door is open. As long as there is breath in our bodies, there is hope for every one of us."

'There is hope Eternal for everyone of us!' This is the teaching that Sri Krishna gives to His dear disciple Arjuna in the Shrimad Bhagavad Gita, "O Arjuna! A person may be completely soiled by sin, he may have committed grave errors, but still he can, walking on the *Gyana marga*, the path of knowledge, attain to sainthood, by the grace of God."

Ambapali, when she heard the Buddha saying this, asked him, "If there is hope for me, then pray tell me, which path should I follow?"

He spoke the *Dharma* to her. She listened to these great words with ears that drank them as the dry earth that has longed for the rain. Mahatma Buddha said to her, "The path is just one and that is, 'Kindle the light within you. *Jyot Jagao! Jyot Jagao!*"

The entire teaching of Mahatma Buddha is summed up in these few words. Each one has to kindle one's own light. For this, each one has to keep a strict watch, a strict vigil on one's mind so that no evil thought, no *vikara* or impure thought stealthily enters the mind. These *vikaras* are like thieves who come to steal our spiritual treasures, yet we embrace these *vikaras* all the time, we are unable to let go of them. Forget giving up desires, we actually keep on multiplying the desires within us. We do not realise that we are behaving like our own enemies. By doing so, we bind ourselves further to this endless wheel of birth and death, which is a circle of endless sorrow and misery.

So the Buddha says to Ambapali, "Kindle the light within you, keep a strict vigil on your mind. Go and serve the poor and the broken ones. Lead a life of sacrifice and service." Sitting at the lotus feet of the Buddha, Ambapali absorbs this teaching, and drinks deeply from the pure and holy vibrations emanating from the peaceful and radiant presence of the Master. Now she experiences a strange peace descending on her mind and soul.

Humbly, she requests him to bless her by accepting food at her house. To the surprise of everyone present, the Buddha graciously accedes to her request.

Ambapali's joy knows no bounds. Her heart is touched by The Buddha's kindness. As she returns home, on the way out of her grove, she sees the princes and aristocrats of Vaishali arriving in their chariots, to meet the Buddha. These princes have also heard of the Buddha's visit and have immense respect for him. They are now on their way to offer their respects to him and to invite him to be their guest for the morrow!

Now, it was the custom in Vaishali, that when the royal chariots passed on the road, the common people would drive their carriages aside to let the princes pass. But today, Ambapali is so imbued with the spirit of devotion, so totally immersed in thinking of the great blessing that has just been bestowed on her, that she fails to extend this courtesy to the princes.

The princes are surprised by this, but not offended; for such is the admiration and affection they have for Ambapali. But one of them calls out to her, "Ambapali, what is the matter with you? You seem to be in such a great hurry, that your chariot has come face to face with our chariots, stopping us in our tracks! You would normally have stopped on one side of the road, as is the custom. What is the cause of this tearing hurry?"

Ambapali replies, "O princes! Please absolve me of this lapse. But I have good cause to be in a hurry. Today is the most blessed day of my life. I have sat at the feet of the Master and listened to his words of wisdom. What is more, he has promised to come with his *sangha* and accept my hospitality in my home tomorrow. Tell me, is this not reason enough for me to make haste? Today my heart is dancing with joy because the Buddha himself has consented to my invitation and will come with his disciples and dine at my house."

The princes are amazed. They say to each other in surprise, "How can this happen? Mahatma Buddha himself belongs to a royal family; how can he accept the invitation for a meal at a courtesan's home?"

Aloud, they say to her, "Now listen to us Ambapali! As soon as we knew that he has come to rest in your gardens, we decided to go and invite him to have food with us at our palace. How can we allow him to accept your hospitality? We will offer you one hundred thousand gold *mohurs*, and in return, you must give us this opportunity of offering him our hospitality. As a citizen of Vaishali, you know you must defer to our wishes. It is our royal prerogative to offer him our hospitality before anyone else."

To this, Ambapali replies, "If you offer me the entire kingdom of Vaishali, with all its subject territories, I would not exchange this great honour of hosting the Buddha, which I have got only due to his divine grace. In all worldly matters, I would defer to your authority and superiority. But this is a matter of my faith and my soul. I cannot deny this chance for your sake. Please forgive me. Now, if you will permit me, I must rush home to make preparations for tomorrow."

The princes are taken aback. But they decide that no matter what she may say, they would still go to the Buddha and convince him to come and have food at the royal palace, instead of dining at a courtesan's place.

They reach the spot where Mahatma Buddha is resting. Bowing their heads at his feet, they request him, "Holy Sire, tomorrow, please sanctify our palace by visiting us and accepting our hospitality."

At this the Buddha says, "That is not possible, because tomorrow I am committed to go to Ambapali's house with my disciples."

The princes exclaim in unison, "What? Ambapali, that prostitute! How can you eat food at a prostitute's house?"

The Buddha replies, "In the court of the Supreme there is no difference between a king and a prostitute, there is no difference between a woman and man. They are all on par. And my dear ones, for me, all of you are equal. May be in the eyes of the world, one is a king and the other is a beggar, one is pure and another is a prostitute, but in my eyes you all are the same, you all are one. In all resides the One Universal spirit!"

The princes are ashamed on hearing these words. Heads bowed, feeling defeated, they bow before the Master and leave for their palace.

That night, Ambapali is unable to sleep due to her excitement. She tells herself, "Mahatma Buddha will himself come and sanctify my home. Henceforth, I shall endeavour to keep my home pure and free from all trace of sin and evil. Never will I commit any deed of impurity in my home. For this house is about to become a temple."

The next day Mahatma Buddha, with his disciples, visits her home. Ambapali welcomes them with devotion, reverence and love in her heart. She serves the Buddha and his brother monks with rice and sweet cakes that she has prepared with her own hands. Having served them to their satisfaction, she sits at his lotus feet and learns the lessons of life, lessons which purify her heart.

Saad sang amolak heera,

Mit gayee sab mann ki peeda!

Has it not been said to us, that in the company of the holy ones and saints, we are given a priceless diamond, which liberates us from the agonies of the mind?

Ambapali says to the Buddha, "I gift my palace and my gardens and all my property to you, and the brothers of your order. I pray you, kindly to accept them. From today all these gardens belong to you. You may build your *kutiya*, your abode, here. Whenever you come to Vaishali, you can come and stay in these gardens."

After this the Buddha leaves Vaishali and moves on. On approaching the age of 80, he tells his disciples, "Now I bid farewell to you all." At that time, his dear, devoted disciple, Ananda was with him, who would always stay ready to serve the master. Ananda himself was a prince. He was the Buddha's step-brother. He had immense respect and faith for his Master. On hearing the words of the Buddha, his eyes fill up with tears. From different parts of India, the Buddha's disciples arrive to have the *antim darshan*, the final vision, of their Master.

Then the Buddha gives them his last message in which he says, "My dear and beloved disciples, keep on putting in your effort, keep striving for the best and one day, surely, you will reap the reward of your efforts. Initially, you may feel that all your hard work, all your efforts are going in vain. In the beginning, when you will try to sit in meditation, your minds will wander. In this manner, may be many years will pass away and you may get disappointed. No, my dear ones, don't get disappointed. Remember, none of your work, none of your efforts go waste. But the reward or fruit of your work comes to you only at the appropriate time. Just like a peasant, a farmer who tills the land and sows the seeds in the fields, waters his fields, but later he has to wait till the appropriate time comes and his field bears the crop. At the right time his field bears the crop, that crop ripens and out of it comes the nourishing wheat. Everything happens at its right time. So, wait for the process, do not get disappointed. Keep on working, keep on striving, and keep on putting in your best efforts. Keep a strict vigil on your minds, make your lives pure. Kindle ye the light, and this light will guide you and take you across the ocean of this world, it will take you to the Other Shore."

With this teaching, the Buddha breathed his last on *Vaisakh Purnima* day, it was the same day when he was born, it was the same *Vaisakh Purnima* day when, sitting under the Bodhi tree, he had attained enlightenment. When the moon was shining in the sky, on the *Vaisakh Purnima* day, that night the Buddha left for his heavenly abode to enter into the Unseen, to attain the *Mahaparinirvan pad*, the Highest State.

Soon thereafter, Ambapali too, renounced her position as a courtesan, accepted the Buddhist faith, and remained till her death, an active supporter of the Buddhist order.

The story of Ambapali reminds us of the lotus flower – which is sacred to Hindu, Jain and Buddhist religious beliefs. The lotus grows in murky water, but it rises on a long stalk, above the surface, in its glorious bloom. This makes the lotus an appropriate symbol of detachment, being unaffected by the surroundings and relationships, either good or bad. Untouched by the impurity of the slime and slush in which it grows, the lotus symbolises the purity of heart and mind. Like the sacred lotus, Ambapali too, managed to rise above her birth and her immoral life, to achieve spiritual evolution with the grace of the Buddha.

Books on Ambapalli

- *Ambapali* by Vimala Raina
- *Ambapali* by Rajesvaraprasad Narayanasimha
- *Buddha's* Wife by Gabriel Constans
- *Buddhist Suttas (Sacred Books of the East)* by F. Max Muller
- *Old Path White Clouds:* Walking in the Footsteps of the Buddha by Thich Nhat Hanh
- *A Dictionary of Buddhism* (Oxford Paperback Reference) by Damien Keown

Karaikkal Ammaiyar

Karaikkal Ammaiyar was born as Punithavathi, heiress to a wealthy trader of South India. The Lord's leela took away from her, the security and comfort of a normal, worldly, married life. She was meant for a higher life, and went on to become one of the great Nayanmars – the venerated Shaivaite saints of Tamilnadu.

Karaikkal Ammaiyar

I have said to my friends again and again: that women saints are no lesser, and in no way inferior in spiritual strength and devotion than their male counterparts. To reinforce this truth, let me now narrate to you, the life of one of the great *Nayanmar* saints of South India – a devoted lady, who became a wandering minstrel, and one of the first poets of Tamil *bhakti* literature.

The sixty-three *nayanmars* were the Shaivaite counterparts of the *Alwars* or great Vaishnava saints of Tamilnadu. The *nayanmars* are thought to have lived between the sixth and tenth century A.D. They came from different castes, different backgrounds and different strata of society. Among them were kings, poets, soldiers, traders and the so-called 'untouchables'. But this they had in common-they were touched with the Lord's divine grace; they were fired by the spark of His love. They were apostles of the *bhakti* movement – they were, without exception, devoted, humble, dedicated followers of Lord Shiva. Occupying pride of place among them is Punithavathi, venerated by countless generations of devotees as Karaikkal Ammaiyar – the mother of Karaikkal.

Karaikkal was a flourishing trading centre and port city in the Chola kingdom of the sixth century A.D. Here lived Dharmadatta, one of the leading merchants in the region, and his wife, Dhanalakshmi. The couple remained childless for long; they performed several austerities and penances, and were blessed with a baby girl, whom they named Punithavathi, meaning *the pure one*. Punithavathi grew up in an environment of devotion and deep adoration for the Lord. The sacred five letter mantra, *Om Namo Shiva* dwelt constantly on her lips, and was deeply imbued in her spirit. She grew up to be a beautiful and charming maiden, well-versed in all the accomplishments expected of a young woman in those days.

Now began the search for the proverbial 'suitable boy' who would not only be a good husband to Punithavathi, but would also understand the tremendous affection that her parents had for her. In other words, someone who would graciously consent to live not too far away from her doting parents. Even such a desirable young man was found for her; he was Paramadatta, son of a rich merchant from the neighbouring city of Nagapattinam. Both sets of parents were delighted with the match; the marriage was celebrated with all pomp and splendour, befitting her father's status as one of the wealthiest merchants of Karaikkal. A splendid mansion was bought for the young couple. The loving father showered the young couple with abundant wealth, for Punithavathi was his only child and heir to his vast fortune. As for young Paramadatta, he was an astute businessman with the capacity for hard work. He soon built up his business to become a leading trader in his own right. He was indeed fortunate to have the love and support of his wife, who was not only an ideal spouse to him, but also continued to cherish her deep devotion for the Lord. She was particularly observant of all the duties expected of a pious *grahasti* – no devotee of the Lord who came to her door was ever turned away without her generous hospitality and charity.

One day, as she was making preparations for the afternoon meal, a servant arrived from her husband's shop. He handed over two luscious mangoes to her; they had been specially brought for Paramadatta by one of his friends. He had sent them home to his wife with the instruction that he would partake of the fruits at lunch. Punithavathi put the mangoes in the *pooja* room, to be offered as *naivedya* to the Lord, and continued with her cooking.

Shortly thereafter, there was a familiar call from outside her door, requesting for *bhiksha* in the name of Lord Shiva. Punithavathi looked out of the window, and saw that it was an ascetic, a wandering devotee of the Lord, quite exhausted and overcome with hunger. He was lean and emaciated; holy ash was smeared all over his body; he sang the name of Lord Shiva incessantly. She was dismayed, because her cooking was still incomplete. How could she send a devotee away from her door without food? Gathering her wits together, she saw that the rice was ready to serve. She gave the ascetic rice and curds, a welcome meal on a hot summer day; and, to make up for the meager meal, she gave one of the mangoes that her husband had sent earlier. Surely her husband would not eat more than one, she thought to herself. Further, he too, would surely appreciate her gesture in offering the other fruit to a devotee of the Lord.

The ascetic ate to his heart's content; he blessed her abundantly and said to her that the sweet and delicious mango had quite revived his flagging energy, and that he would now proceed on his pilgrimage. Punithavathi touched his feet and sought his blessings before he went away.

It was mid-day soon; and Paramadatta returned home for lunch. Having washed his hands and feet, he bowed before the image of the Lord, before sitting down to lunch. Punithavathi served him with love and care. When the meal was over, he said to her, "Bring me one of those mangoes I sent home today."

Punithavathi brought the mango and served it to her husband. "I have offered it to the Lord as *naivedya*," she informed her husband, as he began to bite into the juicy mango.

Paramadatta took his time to enjoy the mango. When he had finished, he said to her, "I have never tasted such a delicious mango in all my life! Can I have the other one as well?"

Punithavathi's heart skipped a beat. Cold sweat broke out on her forehead. What could she do now? Should she tell her husband that she had given the second mango away as *bhiksha*? Surely he would understand that an ascetic should not be sent away hungry from their door? On the other hand, had he not clearly sent instructions that he would eat the mangoes at lunch? What would he say if he realised that his wife had disobeyed him, ignored his instructions and given away the fruit in charity? Could this not be construed as carelessness, heedlessness and lack of respect for him?

With trembling hands, with tear-filled eyes, Punithavathi stepped into the *pooja* room. "Lord, You have never ever let down Your devoted servants," she prayed to Shiva. "I beg You to help me in my distress. You know I never meant disrespect to my husband. You know too, that I offered it to a devotee in whom I beheld Your image. Please show me a way out of this distressing situation now."

Miraculously, a large and luscious mango manifested itself in her hand! Breathless with gratitude, she thanked the Lord, wiped her tears away, and hastily placed the fruit before her husband.

Paramadatta tasted the mango and stopped short for a moment, as if taken by surprise. After a few seconds, he bit into the mango again, and his expression grew thoughtful. He put the fruit down, and gazed into his wife's eyes. "Is this one of the fruits I sent you this morning?" he asked her.

Punithavathi swallowed hard. "Yes it is..." she stammered in confusion. "There are no other mangoes in the house except the ones you sent this morning."

Paramadatta stared at her. "Tell me the truth," he said to her coldly. "This is just not the same as the fruit I ate earlier. It tastes different... it smells different... it does not seem as if it is a local breed of mango at all! Where did you get it from?"

His wife now began to tremble. "I... I didn't get it... I brought it from the *pooja* room where I had left it earlier... I did not give it away... no one got it for me."

Paramadatta's eyes narrowed in suspicion. "Where did you get the fruit from?" he asked again. "Who gave you this fruit? I know this is not the same as the one I ate earlier; that one was good; but this one is ambrosial! It cannot have come from these parts. So I am asking you to tell me, who gave it to you? Who brought it for you?"

"Beloved, who would bring fruits for me? Where would I go looking for mangoes?"

"I don't know. That is exactly what I am asking you to tell me. This is not the mango I sent you. So I want to know, what happened to the mango I sent this morning? And where did this one come from? I order you to tell me the truth. As your husband, it is my right to know what is going on here. If you do not answer my question, I will most certainly be angry and upset –

and let me tell you, your words and demeanour have already aroused my suspicions."

Strange are the ways of fate, we say time and again. An everyday occurrence, a wife serving a meal to her husband, was fast turning into a nightmare. What could he be thinking? Was he afraid? Was he puzzled? Was he suspicious? Was he jealous? Who can tell?

Punithavathi broke down into sobs and fell at his feet. "Oh my beloved one, forgive me!" she exclaimed. "Forgive your foolish wife – for I gave away one of the mangoes to a Shiva *bhakta* who came to our door for *bhiksha*."

"You gave away the fruit I sent; you gave it to a beggar," her husband responded coldly. "That is half the truth; I still need to know where the second mango came from. When I asked for it, you trembled and turned pale. Only after a lapse of few minutes was this mango brought to me. So what was the reluctance all about?"

"Dear husband, do not doubt my faith," cried the distraught lady. "I was so afraid that you would be angry, that I prayed to Lord Shiva to help me in my distress. It was He who put this mango into my hand."

"What? The Lord put this mango into your hand? Do you really want me to believe that?"

"Believe it if you will, for I have no other support, no other saviour, except the Lord. To whom can a distressed soul turn, but to Him who is the Protector of all souls? He it was who put this mango into my hand."

"Well then, Punitha, let Him do so once again, here and now, before my own eyes, so that I can get to the bottom of this strange mystery. Get me another mango – from the Lord – just like this one on my plate."

"How can we put the Lord to the test in this manner?" cried Punithavathi. "You are my husband; you have every right to question me or mistrust me. But the Lord is above our questions and trust! We cannot call Him to stand testimony to our words and actions."

"That is exactly what your Lord must do, if I am not to draw my own conclusions about your conduct and character. You must know you have aroused my worst suspicions with that impossible story. Now, it is up to you to prove it – and to place yourself above suspicion!"

Punithavathi was forlorn and deeply distressed. "O, Lord, O Parameshwara, O merciful and compassionate One!" she cried. "Clear my husband's mistrust and suspicion. Save me from this harrowing situation where my word, nay, my conduct is questioned. Prove to my dear husband that it was indeed You, Lord of Kailash, Lord of the mighty *trishul*, destroyer of all evil, who gave me that mango! I beseech you, Shankara, save Your wretched servant from this dishonour that is imputed to her!"

Lo and behold, a luscious golden mango appeared forthwith in her outstretched hand! Immediately, she placed it in her husband's hand. No sooner did he receive it, than it disappeared before his very eyes!

Her husband was stunned! His narrow suspicions were dispelled by a wave of fear and awe. This was no ordinary young woman whom he had married! He had treated her as a subordinate, as a lowly creature meant to serve him and fulfill his every need. But she was an extraordinary mortal, someone who spoke to God, and called on Him to support her and come to her aid whenever she needed His help! And God heard her, and fulfilled her every whim! No wonder the mango had tasted divine! It was not grown upon this earth! As for himself, what had he been doing? He had been living with a saint of the Lord! He had ordered her about, spoken to her curtly, expected her to wait on him, serve him and cater to his whims and fancies! What a wretched sinner he was!

Then and there Paramadatta fell at her feet. "Forgive me, O saint of God!" he cried. "I have been an ignorant wretch! I have treated you as a worldly creature, as my wife and bonded servant. I humbly request you to forgive me and release me from this unnatural bondage in which I have placed myself."

Punithavathi was stunned. She was, at heart, a simple, innocent woman. She had been taught that her husband was her Lord and Master, and that the purpose of her life was to love him, serve him, and obey him. Here he was, falling at her feet! Her distress was acute. "Beloved, don't talk to me thus!" she cried. "You know I am, and always will be, your slave and servant!"

"Profanity!" he cried out. "Pray do not add to my burden of sins. I was living in illusion till now. You have opened my eyes. From now, I will no longer impose myself on your saintly life. You are a divine being, a chosen saint of God. I am a mere mortal. I shall vanish from your life forever, and try to atone for my sins!"

With those words, he walked out of the house, out of Karaikkal and was never to be seen again in the city.

Young and beautiful, Punithavathi was abandoned and forsaken. Her family tried their best to trace her husband's whereabouts. Many years passed. It was rumoured that he had shifted to the Pandya kingdom. They went after him, taking Punithavathi with them. Alas, they found him married to another girl, and he had a daughter called Punithavathi!

Confronted by her family, he shocked them by falling at Punithavathi's feet and asking her to bless his wife and child. "Do not yoke this saint with a lowly mortal like me," he begged her relatives. "She is a saint of God, and I am an abject sinner. I can only worship her, I cannot be her spouse, for I am unfit to be her equal."

Tears of anguish and sorrow flowed from Punithavathi's eyes. Her small and simple world of marriage and domesticity came crashing all around her. What could she do? Who would be her support in the years to come? And all for what – for an act of charity! She realised that she was witnessing, nay, participating in the Lord's *leela!*

"Alas, poor young thing, what will she do now?" wailed her distraught relatives. "Such youth and such beauty, and no one to share her life with! What will become of her?"

"Dear Lord, it is Thy Will that I should be isolated thus from family bonds," she said to herself. "I accept Your Will. I only ask that you wipe away my youthful form, and grace me with the face and figure of old age."

The Lord of *Mrityunjaya* granted her wish, and she was immediately turned into a ghostly, skeletal form, a bag of bones far, far removed from the beautiful woman who had stood there just moments ago!

Her family too, fell at her feet now. They were too frightened and confused to understand what was happening to her.

Now, she set out on a journey to Mount Kailash, determined to have the *darshan* of her Lord and Protector. It is said that when she reached the sacred mountain, she felt it would be wrong to put her foot on it, and therefore, she climbed the mountain on her head!

When Parvati saw this spectacle, she could not believe her eyes! She called out to her consort, Lord Shiva, that a skeletal form was climbing up Mount Kailash on its head. Shiva assured her that it was one of his greatest devotees, who had had the skeletal form as a boon from him. With these words, He rushed out to meet the saint, and exclaimed on seeing her, "*Ammaiye!*" (O, Mother!)

Thus did Punithavathi become Karaikkal Ammaiyar. She spent the rest of her life wandering all over the land, visiting famous temples and shrines, and singing songs in praise of Lord Shiva. Her songs are treasured in Tamil literature and in the *bhakti* tradition of music. To this day, devotees in Karaikkal celebrate the great mango festival, which commemorates the miraculous event that transformed her life. Curd, rice and mangoes are distributed to all devotees in memory of that transforming event in the saint's life. In every temple dedicated to Shiva, you will find Karaikkal Ammaiyar among the *nayanmar* saints; and her songs are held as jewels of Tamil devotional literature.

Sayings by Karaikkal Ammaiyar

O heart! Avoid abiding here all wilted and scared
And reduced to bones (when) assailed by the sweeping
Onslaught of cruel misery; hail Him unwearied;
He is the Lord-God whose crest is adorned
With the Ganga that flows dashing against its banks,
The white crepuscular crescent and the madar flower.

* * * * *

If you die, your noble kin will pile up dead wood and burn you;
O heart like unto the sea, while yet alive live loftily;
Listen with zest to the glory of Him — the Bather in ghee
Who ate the venom of the vast sea — and stand redeemed.

* * * * *

After my birth, since the hour I began to cultivate
Words, I but contemplated Your Lotus Feet
In excelling love, O blue-throated Lord-God
Of the celestials, when will you uproot my misery?
My misery He may not uproot; pity me He may not; neither
May He reveal to me the way; yet for our Lord
Whose form is Light, and who decked with bones, dances
In the fire, my heart's love shall never suffer decrease.
In each birth we take we are His servants alone;
For ever our love is vouchsafed to Him only; we will serve none
But Him, the One of dense, matted hair who sports
An indivisible chip of the moon. May You rule us for ever.

Books by Karaikkal Ammaiyar

- *Arbhuta Tiru Antadi:* poem of 100 verses in praise of Lord Shiva

Books on Karaikkal Ammaiyar

- The Life and Mission of *Karaikkal* Ammaiyar Jagadeesan, N Bhattacharya, N.N. *[ed]* Medieval Bhakti Movements in India *Munishiram Manoharlal*
- *Karaikkalammaiyar: Part 1: An iconographical and textual study; Part 2: Poems for Siva* by Peter de Bruijn
- *Sixty-Three Nayanmar Saints* by Swami Shivananda
- *Dictionary of Hindu Lore and Legend* by Anna Dhallapiccola
- *Karaikkal Ammaiyar (Publication / International Institute* of *Tamil Studies)* by Cacivalli
- *Karaikkal Ammaiyar: Valvum ilakkiyamum* by Janaka Cuntaram
- *Karaikkal Ammaiyar: Icai natakam* by Papanacam Civan

Sri Vallabhacharya

Sri Vallabhacharya is venerated as the last of the four great Vaishnava acharyas who established the various Vaishnava schools of thought based on Vedantic philosophy. An exceptionally gifted child prodigy, he was widely acclaimed as Bala Saraswati, and venerated as a guru in his own time. In the tradition of the great acharyas before him, Sri Vallabha also wrote his interpretation and commentary on sacred scriptures, and preached his message of pushti marga to his followers.

Sri Vallabhacharya

*T*he Hindu faith has produced four great *acharyas*. In the earlier volumes of this collection on Saints, we have already read concerning – Sri Adi Shankara Acharya and Sri Ramanuja Acharya. The third *acharya* was Sri Vallabha Acharya. These great *acharyas* were recognised as *aavatara purushas* in their own time.

The word *acharya* in Sanskrit means a Holy teacher, a spiritual guide or preceptor. The *acharyas* became the founders of distinct sects of Hinduism, which still follow their precepts and teachings. However, it must be emphasised that all the great *acharyas* recognise the fundamental authority of the main Hindu scriptures – the *Vedanta*, the *Sutras*, the *Upanishads* and the *Bhagavad Gita*.

Though the words *Guru* and *Acharya* are used interchangeably, there is a distinction between the two. The *acharya* adopts the *shastras* or rules of a particular *sampradhaya* or tradition. We now refer to these as sects or sub-sects within Hinduism. As we know, the Hindu tradition consists of several sects, which enjoin a particular code of conduct on their followers: thus we have Shaivism, Vaishnavism and the Madhva tradition; we also have the lineage of great leaders like Sri Chaitanya, Sri Ramakrishna and others. For each of these traditions there are holy texts, codes of conduct to be adhered to by their followers.

An *acharya* belonging to any tradition must be one who is well versed in the *shastras* of that particular tradition; and he must conduct himself according to these rules and precepts, and also pass these rules on to his followers and disciples. Thus we have the twin terms, *shastra* – *sampradaya* (rule and tradition) and *achara* – *anushtana* (conducts and rituals).

A spiritual leader who lives a disciplined life according to the rules, customs and practices of the particular tradition or *sampradhaya* to which he belongs, is an *Acharya*. He must also pass on these rules and customs to his disciples, belonging to the same *sampradhaya*. An *acharya* thus represents a system – a particular *shastraic* tradition. He must have systematically studied the great works and texts of that tradition; he must teach the same systematically to his disciples.

We will do well to remember that the great *acharyas* – Adi Shankara, Ramanuja, Vallabha and Madhva – were *also* regarded as Gurus and learnt at the feet of their own Gurus!

Sri Vallabhacharya is venerated as the last of the four great Vaishnava *acharyas* who established the various Vaishnava schools of thought based on Vedantic philosophy. His three distinguished predecessors being Sri Ramanujacharya, Sri Madhvacharya and Sri Nimbarkacharya.

Sri Vallabha is today widely venerated in Western India – particularly in Gujarat and Rajasthan. But we know that saints belong to all people, all regions and races! Thus, some records tell us that he was actually born in a family of pious Telugu Vaishnavas. His ancestor Yagnanarayana Bhatta, had been granted a special boon by Sri Krishna – that He Himself would take birth in their family as an *avatara purusha*, when he and his descendants had completed the performance of one hundred *somayagnas*. This task was accomplished during the lifetime of his descendant, Lakshmana Bhatta, who had migrated to the holy town of Varanasi. It is thought that Sri Vallabha was born in the forests of Champaranya in the year 1479 to Lakshmana Bhatta and his wife Illamma.

A thrilling account is given of the miraculous birth of Sri Vallabhacharya. Those were dark days in North India when Hindus were often attacked and persecuted by Mughal soldiers. Many Hindus migrated from their hometowns to escape the forced conversions imposed on them by the rulers. Under this threat Lakshmana Bhatta and his wife had to leave Varanasi urgently. As he and his pregnant wife were crossing the Champaranya forest, the lady took ill, and they were forced to seek shelter under a tree in the densely wooded region. Unable to withstand the physical and emotional stress and strain of the ordeal, the young mother delivered a premature baby, which showed no signs of life whatever! It did not move or cry or even open its eyes. Deeply saddened, the parents wrapped the baby in a cloth and left it under the tree, and went to look for help. It is said that Sri Krishna appeared before them in a vision and asked them to go back to their baby: upon their return, they found their infant, alive and well – guarded from the wild animals in the forest by a ring of fire all around him! The mother eagerly put her arms through the fire, unscathed, and picked up her child. They named him Vallabha, meaning, 'the dear one', in Sanskrit.

Vallabha was a prodigy, an exceptionally gifted child. Blessed with great innate abilities, he mastered the ancient scriptures at a young age. Not only did he master the four Vedas, the *Aghamas* and *Puranas*, but also drank deeply at the fount of Hindu philosophy of the great *acharyas* before him. His study also extended to cover Buddhist and Jain schools of thought. Little wonder then, that he was widely acclaimed as *Bala Saraswati* – a title reserved for divinely inspired children.

When the great King Krishna Devaraya came to the throne of the Vijayanagar Kingdom, an impressive assembly of scholars were called to his court to discuss the nature of Brahman – whether he was dualistic or non-dualistic. It is said that the debate lasted for over four weeks. Vallabha participated in the discussion, considering the invitation as a divine command. It was he who emerged as the winner, propounding his own philosophy of *shuddha dvaita* or pure dualism, with his profound knowledge and wisdom, and his superior powers of elocution and persuasion. The day of his victory was celebrated as a victory for the entire Vaishnava tradition. It was in this august gathering that Krishna Devaraya conferred on him the title of Jagadguru, along with a gift of hundred *maunds* of gold, in a *kanakabishekam* (shower of gold) ceremony. Vallabha gave all the gold away to poor people, retaining only seven *mohurs* for himself – and this, to offer as ornaments to his personal deity.

Now began a period of pilgrimages across the length and breath of our ancient land. Vallabha considered it his duty, nay, his life's mission, to preach on the sacred texts of Hinduism. It is thought that he delivered discourses on the Shrimad Bhagavatam at no less than eighty-four centres – from Kedarnath in the North, to Rameshwaram in the South.

These are today visited by the devout as the sacred *Chaurasi bhaitak*.

It was Vallabha's earnest desire to remain a celibate, adhering to the *vrata* of *brahmacharya*. To this end, he never wore stitched clothes; he only wore a simple dhoti and an *angavastra* or upper cloth; wherever he went, he always walked barefoot; he always stayed away from crowds, in suburbs and outside villages. However, it is thought that his guru, Sri Vittalanandha of

Pandharpur, commanded him to take up the life of *grihastashrama;* accordingly he took as his wife, a pious lady called Mahalakshmi. They were blessed with two sons, Gopinath and Vittalnath. Just before the birth of his children, he had a beautiful vision of Balrama and Sri Krishna, coming to play with him on the banks of the river Yamuna. From then on, he regarded his sons as images of Balrama and Sri Krishna.

Many were the miraculous events the Lord enacted in Vallabha's life. Once, Sri Krishna appeared to him in a dream, and ordered him to proceed to Govardhan hill in Vrijbhoomi, where He, the Lord, had spent his childhood days as Bal Krishna. On reaching this sacred destination, Vallabha was blessed with a vision of Krishna as Srinaathji, and a sacred *mantra* was also given to him by the Lord, to initiate his disciples. His devout disciple, Damodar Das became the first to be initiated by Vallabha. Thousands of others followed, and soon Vallabha became a venerated *acharya*, preaching his message of *pushti marga* to his followers.

In the tradition of the great *acharyas* before him, Sri Vallabha also wrote his interpretation and commentary on sacred scriptures like the *Brahmasutra*, the Bhagavad Gita and the Upanishads. People then began to refer to him as Sri Vallabhacharya. His works include the *Vyasa Sutra Bhashya, Jaimini Sutra Bhasya, Bhagavata Tika Subodhini, Pushti Pravala Maryada* and *Siddhanta Rahasya*. All these books are in Sanskrit. He also wrote many books in Brij Bhasha.

Also, in order to help seekers on the path of *pushti marga*, (the path of grace), he wrote sixteen beautiful poems which we know today as the *Shodasha Granthas*. They urge us to attain Sri Krishna through *Seva* (service) and *Smarana* (remembering). The central message of the *Shodasha Granthas* is absolute and utter surrender to the Lord.

Like the great sages before him, he too, travelled across the length and breath of India, visiting several sacred sites of pilgrimage. Wherever he went, he impressed Kings and commoners alike, with his brilliant intellect and profound philosophy of *shudha dvaita*.

His fame and respect grew with years, and he spread devotion for the Lord among thousands of people. When his sons were old enough to manage their affairs, he renounced the world. Soon thereafter, he departed this earth, by immersing his physical body in the holy waters of the Ganga. People saw a brilliant flame ascend towards heaven, as he entered the Ganga.

Sri Vallabhacharya propounded the philosophy of *shuddha dvaita* or pure monism. This stands between the *advaita* of Sri Shankara and the *visishtadvaita* of Sri Ramanuja. *Shuddha dvaita* views the world of men and matter as real – for God has created it. The soul of man is a subtle form of *Brahman*, which remains unchanged by the influence of *maya*.

His religion is addressed to the worship of Sri Krishna, and is profoundly influenced by Sri Ramanuja.

His personal God is Sri Krishna, whom he describes as *Purushottama* (Supreme One). Sri Vallabha argues that *bhakti* or devotion is the chief means of liberation, but he also emphasises the value of *anugraha* (grace) and *gnana* (wisdom). *Jiva*, or the soul of man, is weakened by sins. God's grace gives *Pushti* (nourishment) and *Poshana* (strength) to the soul. Therefore, Sri Vallabha's way of devotion is known as the *Pushti Marga* (the way of nourishment through grace)'.

Blessed be his name!

Sayings of Vallabha Acharya

Which religion gives the greatest joy to God? That which inspires human beings to practice *Ahimsa* and compassion to all creatures.
(His) lips are sweet
(His) face is sweet
(His) eyes are sweet
(His) smile is sweet
(His) heart is sweet
(His) gait (walk) is sweet
Everything is sweet about the Lord of Sweetness
(His) words are sweet
(His) character and deeds are sweet
(His) dress (garment) is sweet
(His) posture is sweet
(His) movements are sweet
(His) wandering is sweet
Everything is sweet about the Lord of Sweetness
(His) flute-playing is sweet
(His) foot-dust is sweet
(His) hands are sweet
(His) feet are sweet
(His) dancing is sweet
(His) friendship (company) is sweet
Everything is sweet about the Lord of Sweetness
(His) song is sweet
(His) drinking is sweet
(His) eating is sweet
(His) sleeping is sweet
(His) beautiful form is sweet
(His) *Tilaka* (Sandalwood paste mark on the forehead) is sweet

Books by Vallabha Acharya

- *Vyasa Sutra Bhashya*
- *Jaimini Sutra Bhasya*
- *Bhagavata Tika Subodhini*
- *Pushti Pravala Maryada*
- *Siddhanta Rahasya*

Books on Vallabha Acharya

- Shuddha-advaita Brahmvaad - Philosophy of Shree Vallabhacharyaji. Kankroli based Shri Vakpati Foundation
- *Lives of Saints* by Swami Sivananda
- *All about Hinduism* by Swami Sivananda
- "Krishna as Loving Husband of God". Alternative Krishnas: Regional and Vernacular Variations on a Hindu Deity - Beck, G.U.Y.L. (2005).
- *Aspects of Medieval Indian Society and Culture.* Ojha, P.N. (1978).
- *Shri Vallabhacharya: His Philosophy and Religion* Shah, J.G. (1969).

Guru Tegh Bahadur

Guru Tegh Bahadur is revered by the faithful as the peerless martyr in the history of the world. The undisputed leader of the Sikhs, he chose to lay down his life for the protection of the *Tilak* and the Sacred Thread of the Hindus. He was a firm believer in the right of the people to freedom of worship. He defied the might and power of Aurangazeb's cruel regime to offer his life as a sacrifice at the altar of freedom from forcible conversion.

Guru Tegh Bahadur

Guru Tegh Bahadur was the ninth Guru of the Sikh faith. He became a *Shaheed*, a martyr, who gave up his life to protect not just himself or his followers, but the devout and pious Hindus of India from forcible conversion.

This great Guru was born in the year 1621, on April 1. He was the youngest son of Guru Hargobind and Bibi Nanki and was born at Amritsar. On birth, he was named Teghmal. Right from his childhood, he was very brave. It is said that from a young age he was trained in the martial arts of swordsmanship and horse riding as well as religious studies by the wise Baba Buddha and Bhai Gurdas, both devoted followers of his father. Muslims attacked the sacred Sikh town of Kartarpur when he was only fourteen (i.e. in the year 1635). The name Tegh Bahadur (mighty of the sword), was bestowed on him by Guru Hargobind after he had shown his valour in a battle with the Mughals.

It is a known fact of history that India has never taken over any country by force. But if any country has attacked India by force, she has faced the enemy bravely. India has never been the aggressor, the first to initiate war.

Once, a great military officer had come to meet Gurudev Sadhu Vaswani. He had a long conversation with Sadhu Vaswani and on leaving, he requested Sadhu Vaswani to give him a teaching that he could take with him. To this Gurudev said, "Love peace within your heart, but keep the powder dry." By this he meant: Let peace prevail in your heart; follow the path of peace always. Do not attack any country but if some other country tries to do the same, then fight back for victory. We should have strong security on the borders in order to protect our motherland. That does not mean that we have the right to attack other countries, but if they attack us, it's our duty to fight back. When Lord Sri Rama defeated Ravana and won over Lanka, He was asked to become the ruler of Lanka. In those days Lanka was rich in gold and it was called 'Swarna Lanka'. Houses in Lanka were made of gold and so was Ravana's entire palace. But Lord Sri Rama declined. He asserted that a son of Lanka deserved to occupy the throne. So Vibhishana was made the King of Lanka. In fact, we know from our reading of the Ramayana, that he was crowned by Sri Rama long before he actually occupied the throne.

So it was that Teghmal, in the tradition of our great country, fought bravely to defend the holy city of the Sikhs from the Mughals, and thus became Tegh Bahadur, the valiant one.

In February 1633 his parents arranged the marriage of Tegh Bahadur with Gujari, daughter of Lal Chand and Bishan Kaur. During his young years Tegh Bahadur had fought bravely alongside his father; but after Guru Hargobind's fierce and bloody battle in 1634 at Kartarpur, he turned to the path of renunciation and meditation. Guru Hargobind now settled down at Kiratpur to live the rest of his life in peace. Tegh Bahadur spent nine years at the holy feet of his father and Guru, before he too chose to settle down at the isolated village of Bakala in 1656 to lead a life of contemplation. He now became known as *Tyag Mal* meaning "the Master of Renunciation". Here Tegh Bahadur would spend many long years in meditation and prayer.

Guru Hargobind did not choose Tegh Bahadur as his successor straightaway; for he felt that the Sikhs needed a strong and forceful leader of men at that point in time – he felt something was still lacking in his young son, who had now chosen a path of renunciation. Instead, Guru Hargobind chose Guru Har Rai, his grandson, as his natural successor. Guru Har Rai in turn chose his youngest son Guru Harkrishan as his successor. When Guru Harkrishan suddenly fell ill at Delhi in 1664, being too weak to move or speak, and fast approaching death, the Guru only said to his followers that his successor was "Baba Bakala". Many Sikhs from

Bakala began to claim that they were the gurus, and it was only after a period of confusion that Tegh Bahadur was accepted as the real Guru. It came to pass this way.

There was a wealthy merchant named Makhan Shah, whose ships carrying valuable cargo, were caught in a fierce storm at sea. He vowed to offer five hundred gold coins to the Guru if his goods reached the shore safely. His wish was fulfilled and his cargo arrived safely at the port. Makhan Shah set out for Delhi to fulfill his vow, only to be told that Guru Harkrishan had passed away and that his successor was at Bakala. Makhan Shah set out for Bakala to pay his homage and the promised amount to the Guru. But when he finally got there, he was confronted with the same quandary as the rest of the Sikhs: who was the real Guru? Being a merchant, Makhan Shah decided that the best way out of the dilemma would be to pay homage to all of the twenty two claimants. Therefore, he went to each one and placed two gold coins before each of them as tribute. When he had visited all of the claimants, a child pointed out to him that a holy man lived across the street. Makhan Shah decided that he may as well pay a tribute to him. When Makhan Shah entered the house he found that Guru Tegh Bahadur was in meditation. He was told that Tegh Bahadur did not like to receive visitors but spent his time in meditation. Makhan Shah waited until he met the Guru and placed two gold coins before him. At this Guru Tegh Bahadur smiled and said to him, "I thought that you had pledged five hundred coins." Makhan Shah was so thrilled that he kissed the Guru's feet and started shouting from the rooftop, "I've found the Guru, I've found the Guru!" All the Sikhs rushed to the house of the quiet saint and when they heard the story, there was much rejoicing all round. Thus it was that the pious, humble saint Tegh Bahadur was acknowledged as being the true Guru of the Sikhs and the natural successor of Guru Harkrishan.

In December 1697, the then king of India, Shahjahan, was an ailing man. Finding that he was now unable to handle the kingdom and its affairs, Shahjahan was apprehensive. He thought of crowning his elder son Dara Shikoh as the king, for Dara was an eligible and worthy successor to the throne after him. Dara Shikoh was indeed a unique and strange individual. A prince by birth, he was truly a *fakir* at heart. He had tremendous faith in the saints and in the holy scriptures. Although he was a Muslim himself, he used to read the Upanishads. He strongly believed that Ishwar, Allah, Waheguru or Sri Rama were all merely different names by which people referred to the One God.

Shahjahan decided to enthrone Dara Shikoh as his successor. Shahjahan's daughter Roshanara wrote a letter to her brother Aurangzeb, who then resided in the Deccan province of South India, informing him about their father's decision to crown his eldest son as the king. This infuriated Aurangzeb. He was of the opinion that Dara Shikoh did not possess adequate knowledge regarding politics as he spent most of his time in the company of saints and sages. Aurangzeb thought that his eldest brother did not have the right to occupy the throne; and if anyone did have the right, it was only himself.

Aurangzeb was only the third in the line of succession to the throne. But he challenged the rule of his father and the succession of Dara Shikoh. He was eventually victorious in the battles that occurred between him and his brothers, and in July 1658, he ascended the throne as Alamgir, although Shahjahan was still alive at that time. He reigned supreme till 1707.

History is a witness to the fact that whenever the thought of 'I' arises in the mind of a ruler, the entire nation has suffered and paid a heavy price. Aurangzeb desired to occupy the royal throne in spite of having two elder brothers who were more eligible successors to the throne than him. He could not forgive his father for not nominating him as the successor. So in a surge of jealousy towards his brother and hatred for his father, he imprisoned his father in the fort of Agra. He inflicted torture on his father while he was in prison.

It is said that one day his father wrote a letter to Aurangzeb saying, "Son, look at the Hindus and see their goodness. They offer water to their ancestors who no longer live. And you! You don't even care to quench your living father's thirst!" To this Aurangzeb replied, "Please do not waste your time writing letters to me as I find them futile. I do not find any reason for you to write me such letters. The water that you used to make ink for this letter could have been used to quench your thirst, if you believe that the water given to you is not enough."

Aurangzeb imprisoned his father for eight long years. The poor former emperor languished in jail and often fell sick. No *hakim* was sent to give him any medicine. In due course he passed away. Aurangzeb's evil intentions led him to poison his elder brother Muradh to have the throne for himself. He was now the absolute ruler of the Kingdom. Later on he also killed his sister Roshanara, his daughter Jabelnisha and two of his sons. Now he was left with only one son, the seven year old Bahadur Shah.

Aurangzeb wanted himself to be considered the greatest among all. Therefore, he sent a vast treasure of diamonds and precious stones to Mecca and Medina. But, the priests there had heard of his cruel and unnatural deeds; hence they refused to accept the precious stones sent by him. This infuriated Aurangzeb, who wished to prove his greatness as a Mughal and a devout Muslim. Therefore, he took the drastic step of announcing that henceforth in India, only one religion – Islam – would be practised. Now began an era of torture and forced conversion of the Hindus of this ancient land. Hindus all over the country were asked to accept Islam as their religion, failing which they would be beheaded. Aurangzeb did not want any temples in his Kingdom. He started destroying the temples and building mosques in their place.

Guru Tegh Bahadur had in the meanwhile, accepted the role of leading the Sikhs and set out on a pilgrimage across the length and breadth of North India, to spread the message of Guru Nanak. Wherever he went the Guru would get wells dug for the people and community kitchens set up. All the offerings he received he gave away to the people, urging them to adopt honesty and hard work and charity as their guiding principles. The Guru now continued his journeys to spread the messages and teachings of Sikhism among the masses across the land. His missionary journey took him to Kurukshetra, Agra, Ittawa, Allahabad and Patna and as far east as Dhaka and Assam. When he finally returned home to Anandpur Sahib in 1672-1673, thousands of devotees flocked to see and hear the Guru.

By now, conditions were rapidly deteriorating for people under the tyrannous rule of emperor Aurangzeb. After ten years of rule, Aurangzeb's dream now was to purge India of all 'infidels' and convert the whole country into a land of Islam. He was an intolerant ruler who had no respect for other religions and launched a brutal campaign of repression. Famous Hindu temples throughout the country were demolished and mosques built in their place. Aurangzeb issued a number of harsh decrees. In 1665 he forbade Hindus to display illuminations at Diwali festivals. In 1668 he forbade Hindu Yatras; in 1671 he issued an order that only Muslims could be landlords of crown lands, and called upon provincial viceroys to dismiss all Hindu clerks. In 1669, he issued a general order calling upon all governors of all provinces to destroy the schools and temples of the 'infidels'; and they were told to put a stop to the teachings and practicing of idolatrous forms of worship. In 1674, lands held by Hindus in Gujarat, in religious grants were all confiscated.

In those days, Kashmiri Pandits were among the most devout and orthodox Hindus in the land. Aurangzeb felt if they could be converted, the rest of the country would easily follow. He did not want to see the *tilak* (holy mark on the forehead) or *janaeu* (sacred thread) on any of his subjects. Unable to withstand the torture meted out to their community by the Muslim Viceroy of Kashmir, the Pandits came in a delegation to meet Guru Tegh Bahadur at Anandpur Sahib.

They said to him, "Guruji, Aurangzeb has sworn that he would behead us if we do not accept Islam. We have asked for a month's time so that we could discuss the issue. We know that you are the present Sikh Guru, therefore, we turn to you for counsel. Please help us."

Guru Tegh Bahadur was deeply moved by their plight. He pondered deeply over the fate of the country that was being subjected to such intolerance and brutality. What could be done to alleviate the people's misery? How should he find a way out of the crisis for the people who had sought him out with such hope and faith?

As the Guru was pondering over the issue, his nine year old son Gobind Rai walked into the room. Struck by the serious and gloomy mood in the room, the young Gobind asked his father what was happening. Guru Tegh Bahadur replied, "Dear son, the Hindus of our country face a deep crisis. Unless a holy man is willing to lay down his life for the sake of religion, there is no hope for their escape from imperial tyranny."

Young Gobind replied instantly, "Revered father, who would be better equipped for this than yourself?"

Guru Tegh Bahadur hugged his son and wept for joy. "I was only worried about the future, for you are far too young," he said to his little son. "Leave me to God," Gobind replied, "and accept the challenge of the Mughals."

On hearing these words from his son, Guru Tegh Bahadur was assured that he no longer needed to worry about his son's future. He then decided to sacrifice his life for the Hindu religion. He told the Kashmiri Pandits to inform Aurangzeb that if Guru Tegh Bahadur adopted Islam, then they and the other Hindus would be ready to follow suit.

On receiving this message, Aurangzeb ordered his soldiers that Guru Tegh Bahadur be immediately brought into his presence. Guru Tegh Bahadur said that he would definitely come to Delhi but only when the time was right for such a visit. He said that he would not be able to come to Delhi with the soldiers, as he had some important work to be done on the way. As soon as the work was done, he would come to Delhi.

Now the Guru went from place to place encouraging people by saying, "You are suffering because you have forgotten God. Now is the time to remember Him. When Dushasan was unrobing Draupadi, she called out to God from the core of her heart saying, *'Tum bin meri kaun khabar le, Govardhan Giridhari'*. When we bow down to the Lotus Feet of the Lord, He comes running to us." He said to the people, "You all have become cowards because you think yourself to be the body. You are not the body that you wear! The body is just an illusion. You are the one residing in the body. No sword can cut it. No fire can burn it. No wind can dry it." In this way Guruji encouraged the people.

Finally he reached Agra. On reaching Agra he sent a message to Aurangzeb saying that he was now ready to come to Delhi. Mughal soldiers captured him and brought him before Aurangzeb, who said to him, "You had better accept Islam, or else you will be beheaded."

To this Guruji replied, "That's the reason I have come here, I won't accept Islam. I would rather sacrifice my life happily instead." Thereafter Guruji was imprisoned. He was locked up in a very tiny cell where he could not even walk around freely.

Guru Tegh Bahadur spent 15 long days in the prison. After 15 days, a Kazi came to Guruji and said, "You are the supreme leader of the Hindus. I give you three options, of which you will be allowed to choose only one. The first one is, accept Islam. The second one is, show a miracle to prove your faith, if you are not willing to accept Islam. The third one if you reject the other two options is, accept death."

The Guru calmly replied, "I will never accept Islam. I won't change my religion. Showing miracles is not our job. We do not have the permission of our Gurus to show miracles. All Sikh Gurus were miracle workers, but they never showed miracles and hence lived a normal, human life. The third choice is of death. That is what I have come here for. I am willing to die. The Mughal Empire has been one of greatest in history. It can't be destroyed otherwise. My death will bring along with it, the death of the Mughal Empire." With these courageous words, Guru Tegh Bahadur warned the Mughals.

It was announced throughout the city that people should get together at Chandni Chowk to witness Guru Tegh Bahadur's death. The next morning, Guru Tegh Bahadur was brought out of the cell. He wished to take a bath before he was executed. So he was taken to a nearby well where he took his bath. He was then brought to Chandni Chowk. At that moment he recited *shlokas* from the Japji Sahib:

Ek Onkar, Satnam, Karta Purakh,

Nirbhau, Nirvair, Akaal Murat, Ajuni Saibhaun,

Gurprasad, Jap

Aad Sach, Jugaad Sach,

Hai Bhi Sach, Nanak Hosi Bhi Sach.

Having recited the entire Japji Sahib he finally uttered the *shloka*:

Jini Naam Dhiaya Gaye Mushkat Ghal

Nanak te Mukh Ujale Kaite chutteh Naal.

Guruji then proceeded towards the Kazi, who ordered his people to behead Guruji. Guruji was beheaded in one stroke. But it is believed by the faithful, that before the sword was lifted to behead Guruji, his head was already miraculously detached from his body.

It is said that the Guru's body was left in the dust as no one dared to pick up the body for fear of the emperor's reprisal. A severe storm swept through the city and under the cover of darkness a Sikh named Bhai Jaita managed to collect the Guru's sacred head and carried it off to Anandpur Sahib to the Guru's son. Another devout Sikh, Bhai Lakhi Shah who had a cart, was able to smuggle the Guru's headless body to his house. Since a public funeral would be too dangerous, Bhai Lakhi Shah cremated the body by setting his house on fire. Meanwhile the head of the Guru was taken to the grief-stricken young Guru Gobind Singh and the widow Mata Gujari. On November 16, 1675 at Anandpur Sahib, a pyre of sandalwood was constructed, sprinkled with roses and the head of Guru Tegh Bahadur was cremated by young Guru Gobind Singh.

Guru Tegh Bahadur is revered by the faithful as the peerless martyr in the history of the world. He laid down his life for the protection of the *Tilak* and the Sacred Thread of the Hindus. He was a firm believer in the right of the people to freedom of worship.

Guru Tegh Bahadur's teachings and philosophy of life are summed up in his hymns. The *shlokas* given at the end of the Holy Granth, which are recited with deep reverence at the conclusion of a Path of the Guru Granth Sahib and on several other occasions, touch the conscience of everyone and remind the devout listeners of the transitory nature of their lives.

Sayings of Guru Tegh Bahadur

This mind does not follow my advice one tiny bit. I am so tired of giving it instructions. It will not refrain from its evil-mindedness. It has gone insane with the intoxication of Maya; it refuses to chant the Lord's praise. Practising deception, it tries to cheat the world. Like a dog's tail, it cannot be straightened; it will not listen to what I tell it. Says Nanak, repeat forever the Name of the Lord, and all your affairs shall be set right.

* * * * *

All things are mere diversions of life: mother, father, siblings, children, relatives and the wife of your home.

* * * * *

When the soul is separated from the body, then they will cry out, calling you a ghost. No one will let you stay, for even half an hour; they drive you out of the house.

* * * * *

The created world is like an illusion, a mirage – see this, reflect upon it in your mind. Says Nanak, repeat forever the Name of the Lord, which shall take you to the Goal.

* * * * *

In this world, I have seen love to be false. Whether they are spouses or friends, all are concerned only with their own happiness.

* * * * *

All say, "Mine, mine", and attach their consciousness to you with love. But at the very last moment, none shall go along with you. How strange are the ways of the world!

* * * * *

The foolish mind has not yet reformed itself, although I have grown weary of continually instructing it. O Nanak, one crosses over the terrifying world-ocean, singing the Songs of Goal."

Books By Guru Tegh Bahadur

- *Contributed many hymns to the Guru Granth Sahib including the Saloks (Mahal 9) near the end of the Guru Granth Sahib*

Books On Guru Tegh Bahadur

- *Guru Tegh Bahadur, prophet and martyr:* A biography by Trilochan Singh
- *Guru Tegh Bahadur: The Sword and the Spirit* by Surinder Singh Kohli
- *Guru Tegh Bahadur (Amar Chitra Katha)* by Anant Pai
- *Eternal Glory of Sri Guru Tegh Bahadur Sahib* by Partap Singh Jaspal
- *Guru Tegh Bahadur* by Harbans Singh
- *Guru Tegh Bahadur: Testimony of conscience (Makers of Indian literature)* by Mohindar Pal Kohli
- *Guru Tegh Bahadur - A Biography* by Surinder Singh Johar
- *Guru Tegh Bahadur: Defender of faith* by Surinder Singh Johar
- *Guru Tegh Bahadur: A study* by B.S. Gupta
- *Guru Tegh Bahadur Martyr and Teacher* by Fauja Singh

*J*ana Bai walked the simple path, the little way of humility and devotion, to attain sainthood. Her life gives us this invaluable message – that to attain God we do not need rites and rituals, nor big talk, nor scriptures. There is no need to go to temples or visit holy places. These are not necessary to attain Him. All we have to remember is the one thing that Jana Bai did – to make God a part of our life. She committed herself only to this one act: to develop the longing for God within her heart. And the Lord accepted the fragrant offering of her devotion and granted her Liberation.

Janabai

*S*even centuries ago, a new wave of *bhakti* – devotion to the Lord – surged across Maharashtra. In different parts of Maharashtra, saints and great souls were born. From among them, many were considered to be Prime teachers and gurus, because they belonged to the upper castes. But there were many saints who were also born in the so-called lower castes. Today, we worship and venerate all these devotees of the Lord alike, for they came upon this earth to teach us the way to true liberation.

I would like to tell you about a *sadhvi*, a saint from Maharashtra. She was not born to wealth and prosperity. She was not literate, for she had not received the benefit of formal education. She could not even read the alphabets, leave alone the *shastras*, or the scriptures.

She was born in what people thought of as a lower caste. Her father's name was Dhama. Since her early days, this child had immense devotion for Vithal, Sri Krishna. Repeatedly she would call out, "Vithoba!

Vithoba!" Again and again, the cry arose from deep within her heart. "Vithoba! Vithoba! When will I attain You? When will I get Your *darshan?*" The little child would pray thus with utmost sincerity.

One day, God appeared in her father's dream and said to him, "Dhama, this girl is not yours. In Pandharpur a *mela*, a fair, is to be held, very soon. Take this girl to the *mela*. You will meet someone, whose name is Dhama Sheth Shimpi, in the *mela*. He is a tailor. You must give your daughter to Dhama Sheth, so that she can go to his house and work for his family. Soon, a saint will be born in his house. This girl is meant to serve the saint and take refuge in him. Now she is only a devotee, but in the course of time, she herself will become a great saint."

Till today, in Pandharpur every year, a fair is organised in which hundreds of thousands of people and devotees from different towns and villages gather together. They are called *'Vaarkaris'*. The devotees set forth from their homes in far-off villages many days prior to the *mela*. They proceed on this pilgrimage on foot, singing the name of Vithoba. "Vithal, Vithal, Panduranga! Vithal, Vithal, Panduranga!" These devotees are totally mesmerised by Vithoba. From one village to another, they walk tirelessly, till they reach Pandharpur at the right time, on the right day – the sacred day of *Aashadi Ekadasi*.

In those days, there was immense faith and devotion in the people. When will such faith and devotion arise in our hearts?

It was at the time of the sacred *Aashadi Ekadasi*, that Dhama Sheth and his group of pilgrims had travelled to Pandharpur for a *darshan* of the Lord. It is said that there were several lakhs of pilgrims who had congregated in Pandharpur for the *darshan* of Vithoba. When, at long last, it was the turn of Dhama Sheth's group to come forward to have a vision of the Lord, they saw a little girl, gazing at Vithoba, while a song poured forth from her lips.

With tears rolling down her cheeks the girl sings, "Where are You residing, My Lord? Come and take me there, so that I can dwell forever with You. I see You, because without Your *darshan* O Vithal, I cannot live. I cannot stay away from You. Please let me know, how I can attain You. This life's breath is being wasted. My Beloved! Without Your *darshan* I cannot survive."

This little seven year old girl was giving vent to the beautiful, pious words and feelings gushing from her heart. As mentioned already, she was illiterate. She had no knowledge of words. That is why she was so fortunate. We educated people are so confused by the books we read. Our talks, our words, are based on books, they are not genuinely from within.

But this girl's words came from deep within her heart. Though she had no knowledge of the scriptures, nature had endowed her with an amazing treasure. This girl was very fond of silence. She would frequently sit in silence and dive into the inner ocean. In silence she would sit and talk to her Beloved, her God. The girl prayed, "My Lord! As each day passes by, I also move forward because one has to move on the path of life. Today, I am standing in front of You, taking Your *darshan*. Shower Your grace on me. It is said, that today is a sacred day, on which You will grant whatever is asked of You. Just give me one blessing. My God, I am not educated, but I do not seek knowledge, nor do I need money or material things. I just need Your Lotus Feet. Lord! I just long for Your *darshan*. Just do me one favour, let me be the first to meet You. Let it be not that I die without Your *darshan*. What if I fail to fulfill the goal of this human birth and I die beforehand? Please pour Your grace on me dear Lord, that before I die, I may attain You. My life's moments are just being wasted until that sacred moment."

Mesmerised by the song and its intense devotion, Dhama Sheth asks, "Who is this girl? Then, the girl's father comes forward to tell him of the dream. They reveal that they have travelled to Pandharpur so that they may hand their little daughter over to Dhama Sheth, a tailor from Narsinghpur, even as the Lord had bade them do.

Dhama Sheth is taken aback. He exclaims, "It is I! I am he whom you seek!" Janabai's father says, "If indeed you are Dhama Sheth, then from today this girl is yours, not mine. She is a devotee of the Lord. In the house where she is to reside, there will be profound grace of God. I have been so instructed, that I should hand her over to you. Please take her with you. She will be like a servant in your house, because we are from a lower caste."

Dhama Sheth brings the girl to Narsingpur. He bestows a lot of love on her. His wife also loves her as a mother. She says, "I am your mother. Don't consider yourself different from us. You can join us in the household work, even as other members of this family do. You too, must consider yourself a member of the family. You are my daughter. Continue to live with us in our house and give us your blessings."

Janabai does the household work, but her heart is with Vithoba. Many times while working, sweet, melodious songs pour out of her lips. Often, while grinding grains or washing clothes, she calls out, "Vithal! Vithal! Many years have passed by, but still I have not had a vision of You."

> If the Ganga flows to the ocean
> And the ocean turns her away,
> Tell me, O Vitthal,
> Who would hear her complaint?

Can the river reject its fish?
Can the mother spurn her child?
Jana says,
Lord,
You must accept those
Who surrender to You.

Everyone of us has such a golden opportunity. In our own homes, we do our allotted task, we share the housework with our spouse or our parents. We serve our husband, our children, we attend to our daily duty. During that time, let us keep remembering God. Keep Him in our mind and keep singing *bhajans*, keep repeating the Name of the Lord. If you do not know *bhajans*, it does not matter. Just keep saying, *"Sri Krishna Arpanam! Sri Krishna Arpanam!"*

Some of Janabai's songs suggest a life of difficult labour in the household, but one that was constantly revived and supported by the strength and power of her intimacy with the Divine:

When Jana sweeps the floor
Her Lord gathers up the dirt.
When she lifts the wooden pestle
He cleans the mortar stone.
He doesn't stand on dignity
He collects cow-pats by her side.
When she goes to fetch the water
Her Lord follows after.

Now Janabai keeps on calling out to her Lord every moment and continues singing. Her songs, her *bhajans* are considered as the priceless treasure of Maharashtra. Even today, in many homes and temples, her *bhajans* are sung with great enthusiasm and devotion. Your eyes will go moist with tears when you listen to her *bhajans*, because they are not merely made up of words, they portray the grief of the aspiring soul and its pure devotion.

Blessed are those eyes, those tears, which flow out of a yearning heart when we repeat the Holy Name of God. Every saint, every realised soul has kept awake at nights and their tears have flowed, in remembering God. When we cry, when we shed tears, it is for worldly desires and passions. Saints have cried due to separation from God. These tears cleanse the heart. Hopefully, such yearning may emerge from our hearts too! Even while working like Janabai, we should keep on remembering God every moment. When such longing for God arises in our heart, then the One whom the Vedas describe as *Ekameva duvityam,* will Himself enter the heart which yearns for Him.

But such intense love does not arise within us, because we are engulfed in ignorance. We are trapped behind the prison bars of *maya* or illusion. Due to the influence of this *maya*, we consider sorrow to be joy, and joy to be sorrow. That is why we feel happy when surrounded by pleasure and enjoyment. We are bound by desires. But, in such pleasure is the seed of sorrow.

We consider the truth as untruth and untruth as truth; the never ending as ending and the ending as never ending. We keep running after shadow shapes of pelf and power and one day, we die. But we remain ignorant about the most important thing and that is, how much God loves us! When humans feel God's love as essential and a benediction, then devotion arises within them and they call out, "O God! I desire only You and I need only You!"

The dream that her father had seen all those years ago, came true. For in Dhama Sheth's house was born a child, who became a great son of Maharashtra, a beloved saint of the people. He was none other than Namdev. Janabai had the golden opportunity to look after him and care for him in his childhood. The many saints and realised souls who came to visit Namdev were also associated with the humble devotee of the Lord, Janabai. She was herself a great soul, a saint-in-the-making; but she was content to regard herself as Namdev's servant – *Naamyasi dasi*, as she herself put it.

In several poems on devotion which she has left behind, she describes herself as "Nama's maid-servant" or "Namdev's Jana". She was one of the closest followers of Namdev and had no ambition other than to serve Namdev and sing the praises of Lord Vithoba. For instance, in one of her poems she sings:

"Let me undergo as many births in this world as You please,

But only grant this — that my desires are fulfilled.
And this is my desire — that I see Pandharpur and serve Namdev in every birth.
Let me be a fowl or a swine, a dog or a cat,
But in each of these lives,
I must see Pandharpur and serve Namdev.
This is the ambition of Namdev's maid.

In another place, Janabai writes:
Give me only this gift, O Hari,
That I shall always sing Your sacred Name.
Fulfill my only desire that You will accept
My humble homage and service.
This is all that I desire.
Have mercy on me and fulfill my desires.
I want to concentrate my eyes and mind on You
And have Your Name on my lips.
For this the maid Jana falls at Your Feet.

One day, she had to grind a huge quantity of *jowar*. That night, after everybody went to bed, she began to grind the grain; and as she toiled over the *chakki*, the philosophy of life poured forth from her lips:

My lovely grindstone —
How sweetly it spins
As I sing your praise.
Come to me, Lord.
Twin poles of World and Spirit

Smooth wooden handles
My five fingers grasp by turns.
Come to me, Lord.
The grindstone of life
Grinds me down like grain.
I gather and pack the flour.
Come to me, Lord.
Spirit heats the vessel,
The scum of sin boils over:
The broth of virtue clears.
Come to me, Lord.
As the grindstone stops, says Jana
So will I, one day. When I go,
The fragrance of my devotion
I'll leave behind.
Come to me, Lord.

It is said that her Lord, Panduranga was so impressed and touched by her devotion and her philosophical rendering of the truth of life, that He came and sat next to her and helped her in her task. He sat beside her, and as they took turns to grind the grain, they discussed various aspects of human life and its struggles.

The day broke and the voices of devotees were heard from a distance. Janabai hastened to bid goodbye to the Lord and urged Him to return to His sanctum sanctorum, before He was missed by the priests at the temple, and the early morning worshippers. As for the Lord, in His hurry, He left behind his silken shawl and His jewelery beside her and covered Himself with Her rug, as he left in a hurry.

When the priests opened the doors what did they see? All the jewels of the deity were missing and in their place was an old, torn rug. Somebody identified it as Janabai's rug. Immediately the priests lodged a complaint against her. A search warrant was issued. The temple authorities rushed to her house – and, sure enough, the Lord's jewels were found beside her grinding stone! She was arrested immediately and the death sentence was passed against her. Namdev's pleadings fell on deaf ears.

Very soon, the day of her execution dawned. She was dragged along the streets to the public execution venue. She was badly injured and bleeding, but nobody cared. She begged the officers not to drag her along, but it was of no avail. Finally, she was brought to the gallows. Her few friends and followers wept bitterly for her but her detractors and a few self seekers gloated over her misery. Little did they know, that the 'low born' maidservant whom they despised, was one who was favoured by the Lord Himself. What does the Lord care about wealth and power and high birth and breeding? For Him, she was a dear devotee, a chosen soul. God chooses such pure souls as His own for their *bhakti*, for the pure love of their hearts, but not for their caste or creed.

Janabai prayed to God in deep anguish, "O God! Why have You allowed Your devotee to be treated so cruelly? Can it be that You are angry with me because I made You do all the household work with me? Dear Lord, did I ever force You to do those menial tasks? Did You not come of Your own accord to talk to me and share my work? How can You ignore me now, when I am being punished for no fault of mine? I am not in the least afraid of death. I know that it will only take me closer to You; but should not the people know that Your humble devotee is not guilty? Should not the world know the truth?"

Turning to the people who were gazing at her, all agog with curiosity, she asked them, "Why have you gathered here? Is this a pleasant spectacle for your entertainment? O, idle folks, go and utter the Name of the Lord, for He alone can save you!"

The dreaded noose was placed around her neck. She was about to be hanged. The name of Panduranga rose in the air and echoed into the sky. The onlookers could not believe their eyes! The rope disappeared and in its place was a beautiful, fragrant garland of flowers around her neck. Janabai was filled with joy. The self seekers hung their heads in shame.

The *Abhanga* written by Sant Namdev appropriately sums up Janabai's greatness –

Janiche Abhanga lihit Narayan |
Karit shravan sadhu sant |

Dhanya techi jani, dhanya tichi bhakti |
Namdev stuti karitisi ||

(Jana's *Abhanga* are composed by God Himself. All the saints listen to her religiously.

Blessed is Jana, blessed is her devotion. Namdev so praises her.)

From Janabai's life, we obtain this teaching, that to attain God we do not need rites and rituals, neither big talk, nor scriptures. There is no need to go to temples or visit holy places. These are not necessary to attain Him. Just remember only one thing, commit yourself only to this one act, develop the longing for God in Your heart. Call out to Him with love and longing. Spend some time in silence, so that you can speak to God and say to Him,

"I love You, God,

I want to love You more and more,

I want to love You more than anything in the world.

I want to love You to distraction, to intoxication,

Grant me pure love, devotion and longing for

Thy Lotus Feet,

And so bless me, that this world bewitching *Maya* may not lead me astray."

This is a very straight and simple way to attain God. Hopefully, such grace may be poured on us so that we can walk on this simple path. We must do our work and fulfill our duty surely, but while doing this work, while fulfilling our duty, while transacting business, let us not forget Him, Who does not forget us even for a moment. Let His name ever be on our lips! Let His vision ever dwell in our hearts! We will indeed be richly blessed.

Sayings of Janabai

If the Ganga flows to the ocean
And the ocean turns her away,
Tell me, O Vitthal,
Who would hear her complaint?

Can the river reject its fish?
Can the mother spurn her child?

Jana says,
Lord,
You must accept those
Who surrender to you.

* * * * *

What I eat is divine
What I drink is divine
My bed is also divine
The divine is here, and it is there
There is nothing empty of divine
Jana says — Vithabai has filled
Everything from the inside out.

Sri Annamacharya

Annamacharya was one of the great singer-saints of the Carnatic tradition, whose immortal songs on the Lord of Tirumala, are treasured by all connoisseurs of devotional music. He is regarded as the *Bishma pitamaha* of Telugu *bhakti sangeet*. Born to pious parents and brought up as a devotee of Lord Balaji, he spent his lifetime singing the glories of the Lord, and spreading the fragrance of his bhakti all around him.

Sri Annamacharya

The saint of whom I am about to speak to you, is regarded as the *Pada-kavita Pitaamaha* (the foremost song-writer and composer) in the *bhakti* tradition of the Telugu language. Sri Annamacharya was born in 1408 and lived a virtuous and blameless life for over ninety years; but it was only in the last century that we came to know about this great saint and his immortal *kritis* or compositions, all of them sung in praise of Balaji or Lord Venkateswara of Tirupati.

Annamacharya was born on the sacred day of *Vaisakh Purnima* in the year 1408 in Tallapaka, a remote village in what is now the Kadappa district of Andhra Pradesh, in South India. It is thought that his ancestors had migrated from Varanasi in North India, due to a severe famine, and were welcomed and helped to settle in the Kingdom of Nanda, thus acquiring the family name of 'Nandavarika'. They were devout *bhaktas* of the Lord, and thus the great singer saint grew up in an environment of piety.

It is said that Sri Annamayya's grandfather, Narayanayya, was a somewhat slow learner; the teacher at the village *gurukul* subjected him to tortuous and cruel drills in order to get him to master a little learning. This had a disastrous effect on the boy's psyche. He decided to put an end to his humiliation and ill-treatment at the hands of his teachers, by taking away his own life.

Gurudev Sadhu Vaswani tells us that the true teacher must always be a friend to his pupils. When children are educated in an environment of love and understanding, the tender and sensitive hearts of the children unfold like flowers, and their personalities bloom. When teachers see themselves as taskmasters, this beautiful bond is destroyed. Even today, we hear of young boys and girls attempting to commit suicide, when they fail to meet with the approval of their teachers or parents. What a great tragedy this is!

Narayanayya too, decided that death was preferable to a life of shame and humiliation. He went to the local temple, where there was a mound which housed a venomous cobra. The villagers worshipped the snake as *naag devata*, and would often offer milk to the snake. The young boy approached the deadly mound; uttering a silent prayer, he put his hand into the opening…

A miracle came to pass at this juncture. The village deity appeared before the boy, and said to him, "Child! You have been given this human birth with a special purpose. Three generations from now, a divine and blessed child will be born in your family. This child will have attributes of Lord Hari, and will grow up to be a saint of the highest order. Therefore, do not yield to despair!"

And so it came to pass. Narayanayya's son, Narayana Suri, and his wife Lakkamamba were without issue for long. They went to offer their prayers at the Tirumala temple. As the couple prostrated before the sacred flag mast or *dwajastamba*, people saw a flash of brilliant light pass from the deity's sword and descend over them. It is therefore believed that the child Annamayya who was born to them soon after, was actually an incarnation of *Nandaka*, the sword of Sri Venkateswara. Annamayya became Annamacharya when he received initiation as a Vaishnava at the hands of his guru at Tirumala.

The young lad had a natural, inborn gift for poetry and song. Even at a very early age, he would often improvise devotional songs in praise of Lord Venkateswara, whom he had chosen as his *ishta devata*. He was always lost in reflection of the Lord, and took hardly any interest in worldly matters. At the age of seven, he left home to try and reach the Lord of the Seven Hills at Tirumala. Then, as now, devotees who climb the Seven Hills, always do so with bare feet, in deference to the sanctity of the location. Annamayya was unaware of this, and had started climbing the hills with his footwear on. Barely had he managed to climb the first hill, when he fell asleep, exhausted.

In a vision, Padmavati, the consort of Balaji, appeared before the young devotee, and lovingly instructed him to go barefoot to have his *darshan* of the Lord. Annamayya awakened from this dream in ecstasy. After an exhilarating climb, he finally reached the temple, whose closed doors opened as if by magic, to let him in. Song after song flowed from his lips, from the fullness of the devotion in his heart. It was here that he met his guru, and received his initiation. His whole life was transformed by his association with holy men, and he began to sing numerous songs in praise of the Lord.

His parents heard of his whereabouts and persuaded him to return home with them. In due course, they entreated him to enter into marriage with a virtuous maiden. God so blessed his marriage, that the young couple were a source of support and inspiration to each other in their spiritual aspirations. It is said that a good wife is God's gift to man. The Lord had indeed blessed his devotee with a soulmate!

Annamayya sought the holy seer of Ahobilam, and received instruction on the great Vaishnava scriptures from him. Although he worshipped Sri Rama, Sri Krishna, Sri Narasimha and Vitthala, he saw all these deities as manifestations of his *ishta devata*, Sri Venkateswara.

He was befriended by a chieftain, Saluva Narasingha, who adopted him as a companion and a respected member of his court. The chieftain was enthralled by Annamayya's divine compositions, and would spend hours, just listening to his friend singing. One day, the saint composed a beautiful hymn in praise of the Lord, on hearing which Narasingha was overwhelmed by the desire to have just such a song sung about himself. He earnestly entreated Annamayya to compose a song on him. Shocked and angered, Annamayya refused outright. "My tongue is accustomed to sing of Mukunda, of Sri Hari," he sang. "I will never utter a word in praise of a mere human."

Enraged, Narasingha ordered his erstwhile friend to be fettered hand and foot and thrown in prison. Bound hand and foot, Annamayya did the only thing that he loved, even in prison: he sang in praise of the Lord. His shackles were broken to fragments, as if by magic!

When this was reported to Narasingha, he ordered the prisoner to be brought before him, and had even stronger shackles put on his hands and feet. "Let me see you break them," he roared in anger. Unperturbed by the King's rage, Annamayya sang his hymn, and the miracle was repeated. Contrite and repentant, Narasingha fell at the feet of the saint and begged his forgiveness. It must be said, to Annamayya's credit, that he readily forgave the chieftain, and continued to treat him as a friend.

From this point in time, Annamayya chose to make Tirumala his abode. Here he continued to compose his songs of devotion, which were carefully inscribed on copper plates by his son, Tirumalayya. These precious copper plates, which eventually came to contain as many as thirty-two thousand *sankirtanas*, were stored in an apartment at the temple, called the *sankirtana bhandara*—the storehouse of songs. The engraved copper plates were found in the Tirumala temple when the secret vault was discovered, just opposite the Hundi, concealed in a very small room. It is said that only 12,000 of the 32,000 *sankirtanas* were found. No leads have been available to trace the remaining songs. It is feared that ignorant persons could have melted the copper plates for personal use.

It is said that Annamacharya, in his old age, met with Saint Purandaradasa, who had come to offer his devotion to the Lord of the seven Hills. The two saints greeted each other lovingly, exchanging tributes. Purandaradasa saw the reflection of Balaji in Annamayya; and the latter saw the saint from Karnataka as an embodiment of Sri Vitthala!

Annamayya's songs are both melodious, and rich in devotion. His songs dwell on the subjects of morality, *Dharma*, righteousness, etc. He has also composed several beautiful songs in the *Madhura bhava*, which still captivate listeners with their lyrical beauty and intensity. Though he sang tens of thousands of songs in praise of several *avataras* of Maha Vishnu, only those on Sri Venkateswara have survived to this day. Well known and popularly acclaimed in his lifetime, they remained mysteriously hidden for over three centuries, until they were discovered in the Twentieth Century.

Even during those days, Annamacharya preached the oneness of all humanity, and refused to submit to distinctions of caste, creed and social status. His song, *Brahmam okate, Parabrahmam okate,* preaches that God is One. He regarded his songs as flowers of devotion at the Lord's Feet. In these immortal songs, he praises Lord Venkateswara, describes his love for him, argues and quarrels with the Lord, confesses the devotee's failures and apprehensions, and surrenders himself utterly to His chosen deity, Venkateshwara. His songs are classified into the *Adhyaatma* (spiritual) and *Sringaara* (romantic) genres.

The authorities of the Tirumala temple and scholars of Sri Venkateswara University have rendered yeoman service to Telugu devotional literature and tradition, by restoring Annamayya's songs and making them popular among the public. There is hardly a home in Andhra, where his lullaby to Balaji, "*Jo Achutananda, jo jo Mukunda!*" is not sung by mothers to put their infants to sleep.

Annamacharya lived till the ripe old age of 95, keeping up his unbroken worship of the Lord through music and song, with at least one composition every day. He died in 1503. Today he is venerated as one of the greatest mystic saints of Andhra.

Books By Annamacharya

- Composed as many as 32,000 sankirtanas (songs) Some popular sankirtanas are:
  - *Adivo alladivo Sri Harivasamu*
  - *Kondalalo nelakonna koneti rayudu vadu*
  - *Bhavamu lona bhahyamu nandunu*
  - *Muddugare Yasoda mungita muthyamu veedu*
  - *Podagantimayya mimmu Purushotthama*
  - *Kanti Sukravaramu gadiya ledinta*
  - *Antharyami alasiti solasiti inthata née sharanune*
  - *Kalaganti kalaganti ippudetu kalaganti*
  - *Eduta evvaru leru antha Vishnu mayame*
  - *Enta mantramuna evvaru talachina*

Books On Annamacharya

- *Annamacharya (Makers of Indian literature)* by Adapa Ramakrishna Rao
- *Shri Annamacharya: A philosophical study : nature of reality and the individual self according to Annamacharya* by H. L Chandrasekhara
- *Annamacharya lyrics of humanism: An anthology of some Annamacharya kirtanas rendered into English* by Tallapaka Annamacharya
- *Annamacharya (T.T.D. religious publications series)* by Kamisetti Srinivasulusetti

Many are the miracles that the Lord works to bring his chosen souls closer to him. When His grace falls on sinners, they are turned into saints. When he casts his glance of mercy on wastrels and philanderers, they realise the value of the gift of this human birth, and turn over a new leaf. The story of **Bilwa Mangal** bears witness to His miraculous power, His infinite compassion and His ever-inspiring leela which are always meant for our benefit.

Bilwa Mangal

The lives of our saints and sages prove to us again and again, that there is no power greater than the grace of God. Devotion to God is the most potent healing and purifying power. When God is in our hearts, when we realise that we need nothing other than His grace, we will find that *mukti* and salvation come to us of their own accord. It was Sant Kabir who taught us that God is not in the temples, or in the mosques, nor on banks of the Ganga or Yamuna rivers; nor is He in Mecca or Medina; God dwells in the hearts of us all. If you want to realise God, all you need to do is cleanse your heart and keep your mind pure. It is not easy, this task of inner purification; but what is impossible for man, is possible with God's grace. This is the great truth, illustrated in the life of the singer saint, which I am about to narrate to you.

It is thought that this saint was born around the end of the Fourteenth Century, in South India. His father was a rich and devout Brahmin named

Ramdas, who named his beloved son Bilwa Mangal, and showered all his love and affection in bringing up the boy according to the prescribed *dharma* of his community. The boy was well educated in Sanskrit; he was given knowledge of the Vedas and other scriptures, and taught to observe all the requisite duties of a good *brahmachari*. This kind of careful upbringing, and the pious environment of his home ensured that Bilwa Mangal grew up to be an ideal youth – kind, compassionate, sweet natured, soft spoken and utterly devoted to God.

Alas! All this idealism and goodness proved to be short-lived. Bilwa Mangal's parents passed away one after the other, while he was still very young. He inherited the considerable wealth of his father at a very early age, and this proved to be the young man's undoing.

Money certainly has its uses, but these uses are beneficial only when man is the master of his wealth, and does not become a slave to it. This is what happened to Bilwa Mangal. As the saying goes, "Too much, too young," may be good for the ego, but it often proves to be detrimental to the spirit. With a great deal of money at his disposal, and no loving father or mother to exercise any control over him, the young man hurtled at breakneck speed towards sin and evil. Unlimited spending power attracted all the wrong kind of 'friends'; 'fair weather friends' who brought with them vices and evil habits. Soon, the pious and devout son of Ramdas became unrecognisable to his few surviving relatives. He was now a dissolute young man, who spent his time drinking, gambling and frequenting houses of ill repute, where his evil-minded friends and newfound women of loose morals dragged him deeper and deeper into the pit of sin.

One evening, he was invited to attend the dance recital of an infamous courtesan called Chintamani. What was meant to be the pastime of an idle evening turned into a lustful passion for Bilwa. He was so enticed, so lured by Chintamani's physical charms, that he lost his mind and heart and body to the woman. He became her abject slave, clinging to her, maddened with lust, and throwing away all his money on her to ensure that she remained his mistress.

To say that he was besotted by her would be to understate his abject condition. It is said: *kamaturanam na bhayam na lajja*. A lustful man knows no fear or shame! Lost to all sense of propriety, decency and decorum, he also lost his sense of reason, logic and all distinction of right and wrong. Physical lust drove all else away, and the young Brahmin became the laughing stock of the town. *Kula dharma*, family honour, social responsibilities – all, all were swept away in the storm of sexual passion. Day and night, he dwelt at Chintamani's house, spending all his waking hours in her company, and dreaming of her charms even when he fell asleep.

One day, a family elder came to remind him that his father's death anniversary was approaching; as the only son, he was bound to perform the *shraadh* ceremony for the departed soul. Chintamani happened to hear this, and said to him, "Go home on the appointed day, and perform the ritual. I do not want to earn the bad *karma* of depriving your ancestors of the *pitru shraadh* that is their due."

Reluctantly, Bilwa Mangal acceded to the elder's request, and promised that he would be at home to perform the ceremony. He gave the old man some money and whispered to him, "Organise whatever needs to be done and keep everything ready for me. I shall perform the required ritual and return to Chintamani's house soon thereafter."

As Chintamani had insisted on it, Bilwa Mangal had no choice but to go home to perform the ceremony. His heart was not in it; mechanically he recited the mantras the priest taught him; like someone in a trance, he offered water and rice to the dead ancestors. Without an appetite, he ate the *prasad*. Blindly, he followed the instructions of the elderly relatives and gave away the alms and *dhaan* required. When the officiating priests left, he said to the elder, "I've done what was required of me. Now, I shall return to my beloved's house."

The old man was scandalised. "What are you thinking? What are you saying?" he protested hotly. "I beseech you, Bilwa Mangal, come to your senses!

Even beasts which lack reason do not give in to such lust! How can you behave in such a revolting manner? Have the decency to consider who you are, and what you owe to the memory of your father. Spend the night here, fasting and praying and keeping a vigil in your father's sacred memory. You cannot be lost to all sense of shame, that you rush to a courtesan's bed so soon after a *shraadh* ceremony!"

The old man's protests were in vain. For Bilwa Mangal was indeed lost to all sense of decency and shame. Angrily, he brushed aside the old man's protests, and set out for Chintamani's house.

The moment he left the house, the weather turned inclement. There was fierce thunder; blinding flashes of lightning lit up the night sky; and the rains came pouring down in a great deluge. But none of this deterred Bilwa, as he rushed to the banks of the river which separated him from his beloved mistress.

"Who is that madman rushing out in this rain?" whispered the villagers, who saw a heedless figure rushing past, with no protection against the wind and the rain. "Why, it is that besotted fool, Bilwa Mangal!" exclaimed a man who recognised him. "I tell you, the demons have taken possession of him! He had just finished performing his father's ceremony, and he is off to fall at the feet of the courtesan. Has anyone ever seen or heard of such shameless conduct?"

Soaked to the skin, shivering in the cold wind, and panting from exertion, Bilwa reached the riverbank, and called out frantically to the boatmen to take him across to the other side. But his pleas fell on deaf ears. The boatmen were busy securing their rafts on the shore, and would not heed his insistent cries.

"Dear friends, name your price, and I shall pay whatever you demand! Take two, three, five gold *mohurs*, but please, oh, please take me across to the other shore!" he cried in desperation.

"You are completely and utterly mad!" the boatmen shouted angrily. "Keep your gold *mohurs* to yourself. We value our lives more than you do, and will not risk crossing the river tonight."

Recklessly, Bilwa plunged into the cold waters of the river. The currents were so powerful that he was almost drowned. But such was the heat of passion, that he began swimming across the river. No matter what happened, he had to reach his beloved Chintamani that night!

In those days, poor villagers who could not afford the funeral expenses of their departed family members, were in the habit of disposing off the dead bodies in the river. One such bloated, rotting corpse came floating in the river. Bilwa, who was completely blinded by the urgency of his lust, hardly saw the corpse for what it was. He clung to it as if it were a raft, and managed to reach the other shore. Climbing out on to the bank, he rushed towards

Chintamani's house, only to find the doors locked and bolted. Chintamani was a 'fallen woman' as respectable people often described her. But even she, in her wildest dreams, could not have imagined that a Brahmin like Bilwa would rush back to her house on the night of his own father's *shraadh* ceremony. She had put out all the lights, secured the doors and gone off to sleep early that night.

Driven by his mad passion, Bilwa saw a creeper outside the bedroom window. He jumped up and caught hold of it and in a minute, entered her bedchamber, crying, "Chinta! My beloved Chinta, here I am, back at your feet where I belong!"

Chintamani awoke with a start. In the dim light of the lamp, she beheld the dishevelled form of her pathetic lover, his clothes tattered, his face like a ghost's apparition, and a foul stench emanating from his body.

"I don't believe it!" she cried in shock and horror. "Are you out of your mind? It is your father's ceremony today. How could you come back here tonight? And pray, how did you manage to cross the river? And how did you manage to enter my house?"

"Oh my dear Chinta," cried Bilwa, still out of breath and exhausted with his inhuman exertion, "I latched myself on to a log of wood and crossed the river; I found a creeper outside your window and climbed up to get into your room. Oh my beloved, did you really think I could stay away from you tonight or any other night?"

Chintamani asked him, "What creeper and what log? And why is such a foul stink emanating from you?" She went out to check for herself, and saw that what Bilwa Mangal had thought was a creeper, was actually a snake. And he had climbed the wall with the help of the snake. Then Chintamani went to the bank of the river and saw what Bilwa Mangal had presumed to be a wooden plank, was in fact a floating corpse immersed into the river by some people.

Shocked and bewildered, she turned to Bilwa Mangal and said, "Aren't you ashamed of what you've done? Open your eyes, young brahmin; it is your father's *shraadh* today. You have forgotten your father who has given you life and everything you own. On such a sacred day, and such a stormy night, you have become demented, you have lost your senses. What have you done? You have taken the support of a corpse and then climbed over the wall with the help of a snake! For what? For the sake of this body, which is made up of flesh and blood; you are infatuated with this body! This body will also turn into a corpse one day. This corpse that you clung on to was perhaps a beautiful girl's body till yesterday. Look at its condition today. O Bilwa Mangal, open your eyes and wake up to the reality of life. If only you would give even a fraction of this desire for my body, which burns within you, to *Shyam Sunder*, Lord Krishna, who is eternally beautiful and whose beauty will never fade! Give Him a bit of your love, and you will be blessed with a new life."

Make no mistake; behind these words spoken by Chintamani, was the grace of God. Each word pierced through the heart of Bilwa Mangal like an arrow. He remembered his father's teachings, and the truths enshrined in the scriptures which he had studied so diligently at one time – was it perhaps in a previous birth?

Have you ever wondered why we have received this human birth? We have got this birth so that through this journey we may meet our long-lost-Beloved, our God! We can reach Him through this human form. We are like the river Ganges which flows continuously, without resting, regardless of the time, regardless of the season, day or night. It only rests when it merges with the sea.

Our life is like the river Ganges; it keeps flowing, without rest. Many brothers and sisters come to meet me and they tell me that they have everything that this life can offer; they have everything this world can give. In spite of it they say they are restless and have no peace of mind. You will not be at rest, because you will not find peace in these external material things.

Rest and peace for the soul do not abide in these outer things. We will get peace only when we merge with the ocean. We will be at peace only when we are able to kiss the feet of our Beloved Lord.

Bilwa Mangal looked back on his life, and was overwrought with all the grief and shame which he had not felt until then. He thought that just to meet the dancing girl, he had committed the obnoxious deed of holding on to a floating corpse, "My father is right now in Heaven," he said to himself. "When I reach the other shore, how will I face him? My father will ask me, what have you done with your life? What reply will I give to him?"

Each word uttered by his mistress had pierced his heart like an arrow and the veil of ignorance was removed from his eyes. Bilwa Mangal fell at the feet of Chintamani and said, "From now on, you are not Chintamani, but you are my mother, because the teaching you have given me today has touched my heart, and I feel that from today, the doors of a new world have opened up for me. I regard you as my Guru." Again he bowed down and took the blessings of Chintamani and said, "Now I shall go in search of *Shyam Sunder*, Sri Krishna Murlidhar and till I find my Beloved, I shall not return."

Bilwa Mangal now becomes a seeker, a *jignasu*. There was only one voice that emanated from the very depths of his being, "My Beloved, where shall I find You? Where shall I go?" Tears flowed from his eyes, as he began to wander in quest of the Lord.

Lo and behold, what comes to pass! As he wanders in quest of liberation, his eyes fall on a beautiful woman approaching. On seeing her, once again, he loses his mind and heart. His good resolutions, his noble intentions are all forgotten. *Shyam Sunder* is forgotten. His mission in life is forgotten. His memory deserts him. He wanders behind the woman, determined to see her face, once again.

Consider the state of a human being. How difficult it is to understand him? Gurudev Sadhu Vaswani often would say, "In every human being there are depths of divinity." On one side, there is the presence of God in every heart. And on the other, there is the filth, the *karmic* residue of our past births. We bring this dirt with us, and often, though it appears that we have been cleansed of it, still some hidden muck is left behind and at certain times it becomes visible. As Bilwa Mangal's sight fell upon this woman, he lost his senses. He forgot his search and thirst for knowledge. He thought to himself, "Who is this beautiful woman?" He started following her like a mad man. The woman was completely unaware of him, and she headed straight for her house. Bilwa Mangal followed her and sat on a stone outside her house. He kept looking towards her house, like a demented man.

Shortly, the owner of the house came out and asked him, "Why are you sitting outside my house? What makes you gaze at the house in such a strange manner? What do you want?" Bilwa Mangal did not attempt to hide anything from him and confessed, "I was passing by, when I saw this beautiful woman. Now I am obsessed by her. I cannot think of anything else. Only one thought prevails in my mind, and that is to keep looking at her beautiful face. I do not wish for anything else."

The owner of the house was an evolved soul, a very kind and compassionate gentleman. Any other man would have driven the crazy stranger away in anger. But, the grace of God made this man say to Bilwa Mangal, "The lady you speak of is my wife. I shall bring her in front of you and you can look at her to your heart's content."

When Bilwa Mangal heard these words, he felt ashamed of himself. That man brought his wife and the innocent lady stood in front of him, bewildered, but Bilwa could not raise his eyes and look at her. Tears of shame and grief and repentance blinded him. Once again he had a change of heart. He felt ashamed of his own condition. He moved away and cried and called out, "O God, what is this? I thought You had blessed me and cleansed me, where did this evil thought come from?"

There were some thorn trees growing nearby. He plucked two thorns from a tree and said, "These eyes are impure, they keep leading me towards sin. It is better to be without these eyes. What is the use of such eyes which make your mind impure and evil?" He pierced his eyes with the thorns and he became blind. That is how Bilwa Mangal came to be called '*soordas*', a person who is blind.

Saints have thought that it is better be blind than to have lustful eyes. It is better to chop off those hands, which, instead of saving others, rob people of their wealth or trouble them. It is better not to have ears than those which listen to gossip.

It is a difficult thing, but it is only when one follows these teachings with resolution and determination, that one can succeed on the spiritual path. Bilwa Mangal pierced his own eyes and became blind. Again he set out on his search. He cried out in agony and longing and finally obtained the *darshan* of Lord Krishna. Whenever he fell or stumbled, Lord Krishna Himself would come and hold his hand and help him. Bilwa Mangal had experienced this miracle a number of times, as he wandered in darkness and despair.

Sri Krishna is a purifier of fallen souls. One has only to call out to Him with a deep feeling of repentance, and He always rushes to our aid. When we genuinely repent, we get purified from within. Then we shall see God. Bilwa Mangal also saw Him. Sri Krishna would take his hand in His and would play with him and then He would suddenly disappear. Sri Krishna plays this game of hide-and-seek with all His devotees. When He hides, His followers call out to Him. In *Soordas's* bhajans, one can get a glimpse of this agony of separation. In one of his songs of devotion, we have words to this effect, "O Sri Krishna, You had held my hand and suddenly You have left it and disappeared. I am helpless and blind and I do not know where You are. What can I do? But I know just one thing, that You have broken my heart. Despite that My Lord, You are always in my heart, and that is due to Your grace. I get Your vision even within my broken heart. I have faith, that because You are so merciful, You won't slip away from my heart. I am blind, my eyes are shut, but I still see Your shining form with me. O my Beloved, may I be sacrificed at your altar again and again, for Your eternal grace is upon me."

Bilwa also begins to sing hymns in praise of the Lord. In his deep devotion, songs are born out of the fire of his spirit, and they are enshrined in the immortal collection called *Krishna Karnamrutam*. When Sri Chaitanya Mahaprabhu visited South India, he read the collection and was deeply moved by the songs. "I treasure these songs as the very jewel of my heart," he remarked. He also wrote a commentary on the songs. The beautiful melody of the songs, and the pure and sweet Sanskrit language in which they are couched, make the *Krishna Karnamrutam* veritably like nectar to the ears, as the title indicates. The songs continue to be sung till today, by Sri Krishna's devotees.

We, too are no better than Bilwa Mangal. If we look within us, we will see that we are stained and filthy. Instead of looking at the faults of others, let us examine and accept our own weaknesses, and call out to God in repentance. Only with God's grace can we be transformed and the Name of God can remain within us as our protective talisman. So call out to God, *"Mohe Apne Hi Rang Mein Rang Lé"*. When God's grace comes upon us, our conscience will be cleansed and our life will be able to fulfill its purpose on earth.

Guru Amar Das

Guru Amardas was not only one of the great gurus of the Sikh faith, but was also one of the standing examples of *guru seva* and *guru bhakti*. His devotion to his Guru was legendary. Having embraced the Sikh faith rather late in his life, he was chosen by his Master, Guru Angad Dev to succeed him as the Guru. He sought the joy of life in serving his master, and this attitude of service and devotion contributed to his spiritual growth. Walking the way of the disciple, he became the true guru, surmounting all obstacles on the seeker's path.

Guru Amar Das

Guru Amar Das was the third of the Ten Gurus of Sikhism. One of the remarkable facts about him was that he became Guru at the age of 73 following in the footsteps of Guru Angad Dev, who passed away in 1552.

Guru Amar Das was born the eldest son of Sri Tej Bhan Bhalla, a farmer and trader; his mother was Mata Lachmi. Both of them were pious Hindus who never failed to make regular pilgrimages to the River Ganga at Haridwar. His family lived in the village of Basarke near Amritsar. Bhai Amar Das was married to Mata Mansa Devi and they had four children – two sons named Bhai Mohan and Bhai Mohri and two daughters named Bibi Dani and Bibi Bhani. (The Guru's younger daughter, Bibi Bhani, later married Bhai Jetha who would become the fourth Sikh Guru, Guru Ram Das.)

In his early life, Bhalla Khatri, as the Guru was then known, lived the life of a very religious Vaishnavite, performing all the ritual pilgrimages and fasts. He often went to Haridwar and Jwalamukhi on pilgrimages and strictly observed all religious rites and ceremonies expected of a devout Hindu. It was not until his old age that he met Guru Angad Dev and converted to the path of Sikhism.

During one of those regular visits to Haridwar, Bhai Amardas happened to meet a *brahmachari*. The two men began to converse, and sat under the shade of a tree to share their lunch. The *brahmachari* was so inspired by Amar Das, that he said to him, "I have never met anyone who is so wise, and yet so kind and gentle and good, as you are! Tell me my friend, who is your Guru?"

Amar Das replied that he did not, actually, have a Guru at that time. On hearing this, the *brahmachari* was shocked and pained. "What have I done?" he exclaimed. "I have shared the food of someone who is not blessed by a Guru! I must return to the Ganga to wash off this sin that I have committed unknowingly." So saying, he left his food half eaten, to retrace his steps to Haridwar.

Amar Das was saddened by the stranger's words. "Alas, the *brahmachari* is right," he said to himself. "When will God lead me to a Guru? When will I be able to surrender myself at the feet of a Master and receive initiation at his holy hands?" Morning and evening, day and night, this aspiration rose from his heart and lips: *"Koi Aan Milave Mera Pritam Pyara..."*

"O, for someone who can unite me with my Beloved...."

Such aspiration is like a cloud that gathers moisture and floats above land. Sooner or later, as we know, the cloud bursts forth as life-giving rain. So it happened with Amar Das. In the blessed shower that resulted from his deep aspiration, he finally met his Guru, when he was well past his sixtieth year!

It is said that Amar Das heard a soulful *kirtan* of the *Gurbani* at the house of his brother, Bhai Manak Chand. The singer was none other than the daughter of Guru Angad Dev, Bibi Amro, who happened to be Manak Chand's daughter-in-law. The words of the holy *Gurbani* captured Amar Das's heart and soul. On enquiry, he was told by his young niece-in-law, that the words were from the sacred scripture of the Sikh faith. The young lady also directed him to meet her father, Guru Angad Dev, at Khadur Sahib. It is recorded that this meeting took place when Amar Das was 61 years old, in 1540.

The meeting was a turning point, indeed, a transforming moment in Amar Das's life. So inspired was he by the Guru's message, that he decided to embrace the Sikh faith then and there. As a devout Sikh, he dedicated himself to the ideal of *seva*, service of the Guru. He began to live at the Guru's ashram. He would rise early in the morning, and bring water from the Beas River for the Guru's bath; he would wash the Guru's clothes and fetch wood from the jungle for the Guru *Langar*. He would stay up late at night, to press the Guru's feet as he fell asleep. He was so dedicated to the *seva* of the

Guru, that he lost all sense of the self. There was not a trace of pride or ego left in him, and so complete was his dedication and commitment, that people simply thought of him as an old man who had no other interest in life. He was called Amru, and generally ignored by all.

Guru Amardas's life is indeed a shining example of *Guru-seva* and *Guru-bhakti*. As already said, he became a disciple of Guru Angad, when he himself was over sixty. The old man sought the joy of his life in serving his Master who was several years younger than him. In the darkness before dawn, he would walk miles to the river Beas in order to fetch a pitcher of fresh water for the Guru's bath – we are told that he would walk *backwards* to the river, so as not to turn his back to the Guru! He would wash the Guru's clothes. He would serve in the Guru's *langar*, doing lowly tasks, rejoicing in utter self-effacement.

Guru Angad watched with interest the spiritual growth of his old disciple. Inwardly, the Guru continued to send him all the grace he needed for his spiritual growth. But outwardly, he was very stern with his disciple; for a disciple must undergo all the rigours of discipline and *seva*. Not for a moment did Amardas resent the seemingly harsh treatment meted out to him by the Guru. Not for a moment did he doubt that the Guru was all love, kindness and mercy. Sometimes, he was not even allowed to come near the Guru. At such times, he would continue to gaze from afar at the Master's face, with the wonder and joy of a child.

A new colony was to be built by the disciples on the bank of the River Beas. The Guru asked Amardas to make his dwelling there. For Amardas, it was sheer death to live away from the physical presence of the Guru; but he did not hesitate. He went to live in Goindwal, the new colony. And every morning, this old man would come, carrying on his grey head, a pitcher of fresh water for the Guru's bath. He would come singing the Guru's *bani* all the way, tears of love and joy flowing out of his aspiring eyes. Thus it was that Amardas walked the way of the true disciple, until he himself became a true Guru, a teacher who brought enlightenment to many.

Guru-*seva* is not just attending to humdrum tasks, menial work allotted by the Guru. Guru-*seva* is not meant for the personal profit or advantage of the Guru—for he is above such needs and wants. Guru-*seva* is a *tapasya*, an austerity which the disciple undertakes for his own spiritual growth and benefit.

Following Guru Angad's attainment of *mukti,* his prime disciple, Guru Amar Das, was nominated by the congregation, as per the Guru's wish, to take up his place as their spiritual mentor. For several years, he had been a devoted disciple of his master rendering personal acts of service to Guru Angad Dev when he had been alive. When he himself succeeded his guru, he was quite an old man, 73 years of age. However, his elevation as the Guru angered many people. Among them was Datu, son of Guru Angad Dev, who proclaimed himself Guru after his father. Datu came to Goindwal to confront Guru Amar Das. He poured his scorn and contempt on the aged Guru.

"You, Amar Das" he said. "You were nothing but a lowly servant in our house when my father lived. You brought water, swept and cleaned the house, washed the clothes and dishes. Now you have ascended to my father's place! You have no right to be here." And in his overweening arrogance and pride, Datu kicked Guru Amar Das.

Old and weak, Guru Amar Das fell down from his seat. But he was no ordinary mortal. Picking himself up from the ground with an effort, the Guru said to Datu, "My dear one! My bones are hard and stiff with age. Your feet must be aching. Let me press them, that you may feel better!"

Such is the mark of saints. They are calm and peaceful, composed and balanced in all states and conditions of life. Their humility makes them beloved of the Lord. The Lord has no need of the learned, the wise, the wealthy and the powerful. He always chooses the lowly and the humble, who have no thought of themselves. He accepts those who with His grace, have completely overcome their ego.

As demanded by Datu, Guru Amar Das left Goindwal the same evening and returned to his native village of Basarke. Here Guru Amar Das shut himself away in a small house, cutting off all contact with the external world, to devote his time to contemplation and meditation. He put up a notice on the front door, which said: "He who opens this door is no Sikh of mine, nor am I his Guru."

A delegation of faithful Sikhs led by Bhai Buddha found the house; seeing the notice on the front door, they cut through the walls to reach the Guru. Bhai Buddha said to the Guru with tear-filled eyes, "Sire! You are our Guru. The Guru being a supreme yogi, cares for nothing in the world – neither fame, nor riches nor a following. But we, your followers, cannot live without your guidance. Guru Angad has tied us to your holy feet. Who will show us the way if not you?"

Touched and moved by their devotion, Guru Amar Das returned to Goindwal. Datu, in the meanwhile, having been unable to gather any followers of his own, had returned to Khadur, quietly relinquishing his claims to be the successor to his father.

Guru Amar Das now made Goindwal his headquarters. Here he made plans to propagate the Sikh faith in a systematic manner. He divided the Sikh Sangat area into 22 preaching centres (*Manjis*), and each was placed under the charge of a devout Sikh. He also visited different parts of India to spread Sikhism, sending out his missionaries to different regions for this purpose.

He strengthened the tradition of *'Guru ka Langar'* and made it compulsory for all visitors to partake of the community meal, saying, *'Pehle Pangat, Phir Sangat'*. It is said that once Emperor Akbar came to see Guru Sahib and he too, had to eat the humble food served in the *langar* before he could have an interview with the Guru. It is also said that the Emperor was so impressed with this system that he expressed his desire to grant some royal property as an endowment for *'Guru ka Langar'*, but the Guru is said to have declined his offer with respect. However, Guru Amar Das persuaded Akbar to waive off the toll-tax (pilgrim's tax) levied on non-Muslims for crossing the Yamuna and Ganga rivers and Akbar did so. The Guru continued to maintain cordial relations with Emperor Akbar.

The Guru preached against Sati and advocated widow-remarriage. He asked the women to discard *'Purdah'* (veil). He introduced new birth, marriage and death ceremonies for the Sikhs. His special gift to the Sikh faith was the collection of prayers called the *Anand Sahib*, which is one of the Five *Banis* recited daily by devout Sikhs.

Guru Amardas Sahib chose his son-in law (Guru) Ramdas to succeed him. He left his physical body at the ripe age of 95 (September 1, 1574) at Goindwal. He left his congregation safe in the hands of his chosen successor, Guru Ramdas Sahib.

Sayings of Guru Amar Das

Without the Guru, man cannot perform *bhakti* and cannot love the Holy Word.

* * * * *

Surrender your body, soul and wealth to the Guru and submit to his Will to win the Lord.

* * * * *

He who has made the mortal sleep shall awaken him. By the Guru's instructions he obtains understanding.

* * * * *

If you walk according to His Will, you shall be like Him whom you serve.

* * * * *

He who soars above the nine gates (organs) and hears the playing of the celestial melody in the Tenth gate, is liberated.

* * * * *

By God's grace, the mortal serves the Guru and through God's grace, the service is performed. By God's grace, the mind is controlled, and by His grace the mind becomes pure.

* * * * *

Man melodies of joy play for one in whose mind the Lord's Name abides.

* * * * *

In the minds of such friends of God is bliss. They reflect over the Guru's hymns, they enshrine the Name of their minds, their pain is dispelled and the Creator blesses them with Divine Light.

* * * * *

O my Soul, supremely sweet is God's Name. It is the destroyer of sins and fears of millions of births. By the Guru's grace, the Unique Lord is seen.

Books by Guru Amar Das

- *Contributed a total of 907 hymns to the Sri Guru Granth Sahib.*
- *Wrote the Anand Sahib, which is one of the Five Banis recited daily by devout Sikhs.*

Books on Guru Amar Das

- *Perspectives on Guru Amar Das* by Singh and Jaggi
- *The widening horizon: Guru Amar Das and his bani* by H. L Agnihotri
- *Guru Amar Das: Life and teachings* by Fauja Singh
- *Thus Spake Guru Amar Das ; A Selection from his Bani in English Rendering* by Gurbachan Singh Talib
- *Peace Lagoon: The Songs of Guru Nanak, Guru Amar Das, Guru Ram Das, Guru Arjun Dev and Guru Gobind Singh: Sacred Songs of the Sikhs* by Sardarni Premka Kaur
- *Guru Amar Das Ji: A biography* by Ranjit Singh
- *Life of Guru Amar Dass Ji* by Jodha Singha

St. Mira

The name of **Mira** lives on in the heart of India, as the symbol of *prema-bhakti*, the loving devotion of Sri Krishna. Born a Rajput princess, and married into a royal family, Mira broke away from age old traditions and hidebound conventions to go out in quest of her spiritual aspiration to find Sri Krishna. Her immortal songs express the longing and love of a heart steeped in Krishna *bhakti.* Mira was a woman who became a *jogen,* a wandering minstrel whose image in our hearts today, is at one with Him whom she adored.

St. Mira

Mira! The princess who turned into a wandering minstrel, the singing saint beloved of thousands of Indians, the devotee of Sri Krishna who turned her back on wealth and pomp and power, to seek liberation and union with the Lord! Her very name is dear to all of us, the devotees of Gurudev Sadhu Vaswani, for Gurudev chose her as a role model for the woman-soul; he chose to name his new educational movement after her. Let me begin this account of Mira's life with his own words:

"Four centuries and a half ago, was born, in a village in Mewar, that spiritual genius, the great singer of the love of God – Saint Mira. She lives in the heart of India. Her songs are so unspeakably rich in the wisdom of the Spirit! Her life was so simple and so sublime!"

"God's saints are shining lights," said a mystic. From the Himalayas to Cape Camorin, from Karachi to Calcutta, Mira is to many a 'shining light'. The secret of her light is devotion (*bhakti*) to Krishna.

In Rajasthan, in Gujarat, and in North India, her songs are still sung in many homes, the central note of the songs being – "I abandon all to Thee, O Lord! To Thee I surrender all I am!"

At a very early age, Sri Krishna put His songs on her lips. She became a flute of the Lord. Some of them I have listened to, again and again, with tear-touched eyes. What a cry pierces the heart when you listen to her songs!

Mira was born around 1499 A.D. She was the daughter of Rana Ratan Singh Rathor, a brave Rajput prince and spirited warrior, who died on the battlefield, fighting Mughul invaders. At a very young age, Mira went to live with her grandfather, Dudaji, in Merta.

The Ranthors of Merta were devout believers in Lord Vishnu. Thus Mira grew up in an atmosphere of intense piety and devotion.

It is said that as a small child, Mira once witnessed a marriage procession, with a richly attired bridegroom, the *dulha*, at the centre of attention, the cynosure of all eyes. So impressed was the little girl that she ran to her mother and asked her in all innocence, "Mother, who is my *dulha*?"

Smiling indulgently at the child, Mira's mother replied, pointing to an image of Sri Krishna, "Here He is, your own *Girdhar Gopal*."

Whether she meant it as a joke or whether she meant it in earnest, who can tell? But from that day onwards, Mira never ever forgot that He was her beloved, her *dulha*, her own *Girdhar Gopal*. She began to regard herself as Sri Krishna's bride.

Morey to Girdhar Gopal, doosro na koyi...

Around this time, a *sadhu* arrived in their palace. He had brought with him, a personal deity, a small image of Sri Krishna to which he offered his *pooja* every morning. No sooner did Mira set eyes on the statue, than she said to her mother, "Mother, could I not have that *murthi*? It is so beautiful that my heart longs to have it as my own."

The indulgent mother asked the *sadhu* if he could give the statue to her daughter. The sadhu politely refused, for it was his *archa murthi*; a visible symbol of the Lord whom he worshipped. However, that very night, he saw Sri Krishna in a vision. The Lord said to him, "You are my true devotee. Won't you please give My *murthi* to Mira?" The following day, the *sadhu* handed the idol over to Mira, and blessed her.

And the little girl was thrilled with her gift! She spent all her time decorating the idol; decking the Lord's image with flowers and ornaments; singing and dancing before Him; talking to Him, and worshipping Him with an intense love and devotion.

Mira's family did not take her devotion seriously. Following the Rajput tradition, they arranged her marriage when she was still very young. The chosen bridegroom was Rana Bhoj Raj, scion of the Royal family of Chittorhgarh. To him was Mira married, with all pomp and splendour. When she left for her husband's home, she was sent with the dowry that was due to a princess; but all that Mira treasured and took with her was the little statue that she had loved and worshipped as a child.

According to some accounts, Mira was a dutiful wife, who did not neglect her household duties. But other accounts reveal that she was reluctant to worship the household deity of her husband's family, and insisted that her devotion was reserved only for Sri Krishna.

Around this time, many parts of Rajputana came under attack from the Mughul sultans of Delhi. In the ensuing struggle between the warlords of Delhi and the fiercely independent Rajput clans, many brave princes lost their lives, Rana Bhoj among them. Around this time, Mira also lost her parents and several of her family members. Perhaps these tragic events taught the young maiden to turn away from the transient, temporal world of material reality and focus her attention on the Eternal. Filled with the spirit of *vairagya,* (detachment) she began to spend all her time at a little shrine of Sri Krishna, that her husband had built for her. Day and night, she sat at the feet of her Beloved Sri Krishna, singing songs in His praise.

The Royal family of Chittorgarh were not pleased with her attitude and her way of life. They had actually expected her to commit *sati*, burning herself alive on her husband's funeral pyre, as was the tradition among Rajput queens. As an alternative to this, they had thought that she would live in seclusion and isolation, as a Rajput widow should, and spend her days in worship of Kali, the deity of their family.

Instead of following these traditional norms, Mira took to a life of ardent worship, becoming one of the leading forces of the great *Bhakti* Movement, sweeping all over medieval India. She openly referred to herself as the Lord's slave, the spouse of Sri Krishna. Like so many saints associated with the *Bhakti* Movement, she ignored petty, parochial divisions of gender, class, caste, and religious boundaries, and spent time caring for the poor. Her true devotion, her divine songs and the sheer spiritual magnetism of her *bhakti*, drew many followers to her temple. They thought that the young princess was the very embodiment of piety. They became Krishna *bhaktas* themselves, and gathered in large numbers to join her *kirtan* and *poojas* at the shrine. Her popularity among the common people grew from more to more. She too, felt she was one of them; for how can there be rich and poor, high and low, prince and pauper, among the lovers of the Lord? If she was a devotee, so were they; if they were servants of Sri Krishna, so was she. They grew to love her, and she mingled with them freely. At times, overcome by her intense devotion, she would even go out on to the streets, stringing her *tanpura*, and dancing in ecstatic piety.

Her brother-in-law, Vikramjit Singh, who had now become the ruler, was displeased by such behaviour, which, he thought, was unbecoming of a Rajput queen. Adding fuel to his fire of wrath was his sister, Uda Bai, who indulged in wild and malicious gossip about Mira. Mira's ever growing popularity among the masses, the great love and reverence in which the people held her, was also a thorn in his flesh. He commanded her to stop dancing and singing in the temple: her reply is in the form of a song whose words are now etched in our hearts:

> Dyed deep am I in the colour of *Shyama*
> To whom I am consecrated,
> Dyed in the colour of Krishna am I.
> I put on my anklets of the love of *Shyama*
> I dance before my *Giridhara*
> Mira is dyed deeply in the colours of Hari.

It is said that he made several attempts to poison her: but each time the poisoned cup was brought to her lips, Sri Krishna turned it into the elixir of life— Mira lived on, for it was the Lord's Will to protect her against all harm.

We have several beautiful stories that have come down to us about this period of her life. One of them concerns her meeting with Sant Ravidas. It is said that it was he, the cobbler saint, who gifted her with his *ektara* and blessed her.

It is also said that Akbar and Tansen, hearing of her devotion and her immortal songs, came in disguise to listen to her, and lost their hearts to her divine music.

At the height of persecution from her in-laws, it is said that Mira sought the advice of her contemporary, Sant Tulsidas, on which course of action she should follow: it is thought that the great poet of the *Ram Charitamanas* advised her that God was greater than family, society and social traditions and that she should never ever give up her devotion to the Lord, no matter what pressures were put on her.

Day after day, Mira faced persecution and psychological pressure from her husband's family. She bore it all in patience, with undaunted courage. In every difficulty and crisis that she faced, her only support and solace was her devotion to Sri Krishna.

The Rana continued his persecution. Once he sent a serpent to the temple; in its place, she found a bunch of flowers for her *pooja*. Soon, there came a stage when Mira decided that she should leave her worldly confines behind her, once and for all. She left Chittor, and set out as a wandering ascetic in search of her Lord.

The princess turned into a *bairagin*, a homeless wanderer.

Gurudev Sadhu Vaswani tells us, that it is ever the fate of those who aspire to meet the Lord, that they must face loneliness; they must tread their chosen path all alone.

Alone, Mira leaves Chittor, in the darkness of the night. Alone, she moves out, this Rajput princess, who is truly heroic at heart, firm in her devotion for Sri Krishna. As Sadhu Vaswani puts it, this is indeed a difficult period in her life – difficult, but blessed. She walks the way of quest, her heart crying out again and again, "Where, O, where art Thou, Beloved?"

Moving along the pilgrim way, she visits shrine after shrine, until she reaches Brindavan. Here she finds a thousand temples dedicated to her dear Sri Krishna. For it was here that He grew up, here that He tended his cows, here that He played the flute, capturing the hearts of the *gopas* and *gopis*, His playmates and beloved companions. Mira's heart is filled with ecstasy!

In Brindavan, she comes to the temple wherein is located the ashram of Jiv Goswami, the great disciple of Sri Chaitanya Mahaprabhu. Mira is anxious to have his *darshan*; standing at the gates of the temple, she sends word that she wishes to pay her respects to the Goswami.

Back comes the prompt reply: "I never meet women!"

Mira smiles. "Foolish me!" she exclaims. "In my ignorance I thought that Sri Krishna was the only male – the *Purushottama* – in Brindavan, while the rest of us were all his *gopis*. Now I know, that He has a peer, a rival, who also considers himself a male in Brindavan!"

Jiv Goswami is unnerved by the statement. He realises that it is no ordinary *bairagin* who stands at his gate. She is a supreme devotee of the Lord. He rises from his seat and rushes out to open the gates of his *kutiya*. With great reverence and admiration he ushers Mira inside. She has opened his eyes to the truth that there can be no bias, no discrimination among the devotees of the Lord.

Wherever she goes, she is greeted by the dwellers of Brindavan with love and joy. "Blessed is Mira!" they sing. "Once a queen, she comes to us as a devotee of Sri Krishna, she comes in the garb of a beggar to mingle with us! Blessed, blessed may she be, forever and forever more!"

As for Mira, she sings in rapture:

And sweep and clean the gardens of Brindavan!
Let me have Thy darshan everyday!
Let me but sing your Name, let me sing the *leela* of Govind,
In the highways and byways of Brindavan!

Let me just be Thy servant, Lord,
Let me only be Thy servant,

After a while, Mira leaves Brindavan, to seek the Lord at Dwaraka. Situated on the sea shore in Kathiawar, is this sacred city, "the city of many gates", built by Sri Krishna Himself, when He walked this earth in the *Dwapara Yuga*. Aptly is it called Dwaraka, for was it not Sri Krishna who promised us that there are many gates to gain access to God, and that He would be there to greet us, by whatever gate we choose to go to Him?

A *mandali* of *bhaktas* gather around the saint, and she spends her days, singing songs in praise of the Lord. One tradition tells us that Rana Vikramjit came to Dwaraka, to seek her forgiveness, and to implore her to return to Chittorgarh. But Mira's mind is made up. She only smiles at him, and is re-absorbed into her *kirtan*.

It is dusk. Mira enters the temple, alone. In silence, she stands before the deity, her own Beloved Lord Krishna. In her heart is a prayer; "More to me than my life art Thou, Beloved! Thou dwellest ever, in my heart, and in my eyes! Be Thou, the breath of my life! Be Thou, the breath of my breath!"

She stretches out her arms to embrace the deity. And the story goes that the deity stretches forth It's arms to welcome her!

Mira falls down in a swoon. Her eyes shed a stream of tears. And Mira's form disappears from the temple. She has merged with the Divine! She has become one with her Lord!

But Mira's songs live on! And she lives on too, in the hearts of all Indians, like the flute of the Lord!

Sayings of St. Mira

Mira's song of the illusion of separateness:-
Forget not this, 0 man!
This human birth is thine,—
A gift from the Blessed One!
But this happens not again and again.
This body is a gift to thee from God
That thou mayst in wisdom grow
And sing in thy heart the Name!
And know this, too, 0 man!
Thou wilt not know the Name
Without the Guru's grace!
Without the Guru thou wilt go athirst.
But with the Guru's aid
A blind man, too, can drink
The nectar of the Name.
So have I found the Lord :
And I sing of Govind, the Gracious One!
And so with faith in Him
I have entered into illumination
And the ecstasy of bliss!
* * * * *
Let my garment be dipped
In colours of the sunset!
Red is my heart
Dyed deep in colour
Of my Lover's love!
So crimson-red let my garment be!
For I go as a bride
To the bowers of the Beloved!
I go to greet Him!
I go to sing to Him my Song,—
The Song of Adoration and Love!

Translated by Gurudev Sadhu Vaswani

Books By St. Mira

- *400 Padas (songs)*
- *Ocean* by Mirabai
- *Sweet on My Lips: The Love Poems of Mirabai* translated by Louise Landes-Levi
- *For Love of the Dark One: Songs of Mirabai* by Mirabai translated by Andrew Schelling

Books On St. Mira

- *The Devotional Poems of Mirabai* by A.J. Alston
- *Mira Bai and Her Padas* by Mirabai and K. P. Bahadur
- *Mira Bai (Rajasthani Poetess)* by Usha S. Nilson
- *The story of Mira Bai* by Bankey Behari
- *The legend of Mira Bai: The Rajput poetess* by M Macauliffe
- *Lives of Saints* by Swami Sivananda
- *St. Mira* by Sadhu T. L. Vaswani
- Mirabai: Ecstatic Poems *by Robert Bly*

Keshub Chandra Sen

Keshub Chandra Sen belonged to a conservative and orthodox family of Bengali Hindus. A contemporary of Maharishi Devendranath Tagore and Sri Ramakrishna Paramahansa, he embraced the Brahmo Samaj, becoming one of its most active members. He studied Christianity in depth, to find that all the great religious teachers were bound together by a common bond. Great was his faith in the Divine mission of the Brahmo Samaj. His contribution to this intellectual, social and spiritual movement was his emphasis on the principle laid down by Rammohan Roy – that service of man was the service of God.

Keshub Chandra Sen

*L*et me take you back to a time when our ancient *sanatana dharma*, the Hindu way of life, was passing through a dark phase. Religion had become dogmatic and ritual-bound, for it was trapped in the control of Brahmins who had lost touch with the spirit of Hinduism, and clung blindly to its rites and rituals. People were so much involved in the externals, the 'rules and regulations' of religion; and many were the cruelties and horrors perpetrated in the name of religion. The barbaric custom of *sati* was preached and practiced in those dark days of the eighteenth century.

I wonder how many are aware of the inhuman custom, which is now thankfully extinct. I shudder even to tell you about it – when a man expired, his wife was decorated in her wedding finery and fresh garlands, and burnt alive on his funeral pyre! She would wail and howl for help; but her cries were drowned in the beating of drums and the loud chants of the crowd who watched the 'miracle' of a *pativrata* (true and loyal wife) mounting up to heaven alive!

This ritual was called 'Sati', and the women who were forced to die in this inhuman manner were worshipped as *sati matas* who would bring glory to their village and community. As I said, those were dark days for our glorious faith. But these hard times also produced their own antidote to such barbarism; and so we had great social reformers like Raja Ram Mohan Roy, founder of Adi, the Brahmo Samaj, who was instrumental in putting an end to sati.

Ram Mohan Roy had travelled to England to represent the case against sati in the British parliament. His plea against the hateful ritual was so powerful, that the British Raj declared sati to be illegal. Roy succeeded in his mission. But his fellow Bengalis did not give him the praise that was his due. They hated him and even threatened to kill him, for they felt he was interfering with matters of their faith. Ram Mohan Roy was undaunted by these threats. He was a great social and religious reformer who lived by the force of his convictions. Unfortunately, death snatched him away before he could return to India; he passed away in England, and is buried at Bristol, where Sadhu Vaswani, as a young pilgrim-delegate to the Welt Congress of religions, went to pay his respects at the sacred Samadhi – a place of sanctity to all members of the Brahmo Samaj.

The holy man of whom I am going to tell you, had a strange link with Ram Mohan Roy. He belonged to an affluent and well-known family of Calcutta, being the grandson of Ramkamal Sen, Diwan of the Calcutta Mint. Ramkamal Sen was one of the leading intellectuals of Bengal, being the compiler of the earliest English-Bengali Dictionary and also the first Indian secretary of the Asiatic society; he was one of the founders of the Hindu College (1817) and the Sanskrit College (1824). The young Keshub therefore received not only an excellent education but also exposure to emerging ideas and philosophies. The grandfather, despite being a great intellectual, was also well known as being a pro-sati Hindu and lifelong *opponent* of Ram Mohan Roy! In fact, his biographers tell us, that the Diwan was responsible for removing Ram Mohan Roy from the Committee of the Hindu College.

Keshub Chandra Sen was born on November 19, 1838. His father, Pyare Mohan Sen had died when he was ten, and young Keshub was brought up by his uncle. As a boy, he attended the Bengali Patshala elementary school and later joined the Hindu College, and Metropolitan College. In 1855, he founded an evening school for the children of working men, which continued till 1858. In 1855, he became the secretary to the Goodwill Fraternity, a Masonic lodge associated with Christian missionaries.

Strange are the ways of destiny! Diwan Ramkamal Sen's grandson, a highly personable man and an eligible young bachelor, began to be attracted to the ideas of the Brahmo Samaj, the very organisation which his family hated and despised! Keshub was married in 1856, and in 1858, he joined the Brahmo Samaj.

As I said to you earlier, Ram Mohan Roy had expired in England in 1833 and his work was taken over by Dwarkanath Tagore, and after him by Debendranath Tagore, who was the father of our great national poet Rabindranath Tagore. The young Keshub Chandra Sen threw himself with great energy and dedication into the work of this society and in 1862, was appointed to take charge of one of its branches. It is said that Maharishi Debendranath Tagore, bestowed on young Keshub, the title Brahmananda (Rejoicer in God) and appointed him as an *acharya* of the society. During this period, he helped to found the Albert College and started the *Indian Mirror*, a weekly journal in which social and moral subjects were discussed, and the pioneering Bengali weekly, *Sulava Samachar*. In 1863 he wrote— *The Brahmo Samaj Vindicated*. He also travelled far and wide, lecturing and preaching.

But this association did not last long. Like many restless young intellectuals of his time, Keshub was, for a brief while, drawn powerfully towards Christianity. Debendranath Tagore advised him against this tendency, and Sen broke away from what he now began to regard as the conservatism of Tagore and the Brahmo Samaj, forming a splinter group called, "Brahmo Samaj of India". He now devoted himself to the task of propagating its doctrines with

missionary zeal. Its tenets at this time were the following:
1. The wide universe is the temple of God.
2. Wisdom is the pure land of pilgrimage.
3. Truth is the everlasting scripture.
4. Faith is the root of all religions.
5. Love is the true spiritual culture.
6. The destruction of selfishness is true asceticism.

In 1866 he delivered an address on *Jesus Christ, Europe and Asia*, which attracted wide attention. It even led people to believe (mistakenly) that he was about to embrace Christianity. He was invited to visit England, where the radical Hindu preacher was warmly welcomed by almost all Christian denominations.

His biographers record that his eloquence, his rhetoric and his complete command of the English language won universal admiration. He was given an audience with the great Queen Victoria, who was quite charmed by the young man and presented him with two autographed books. It is recorded too, that Max Muller, who met him during this tour, urged him to convert to Christianity, once and for all. However, Keshub was disappointed by the religious atmosphere in England. Christianity in England appeared to him too sectarian and narrow and Christian life itself, more materialistic and outward than spiritual and inward. "I came here an Indian, I go back a confirmed Indian; I came here a Theist, I go back a confirmed Theist. I have learnt to love my own country more and more." These words spoken at the farewell function may probably help us understand his disillusion and disappointment with the Christian church.

However, he continued to be influenced by Christian rites and beliefs, even after his return to India. He now began to develop a tendency towards mysticism and a greater leaning to the spiritual teaching of the Indian philosophies, as well as a somewhat despotic attitude towards the Samaj. What came as the last straw was Sen's decision to marry his thirteen year old daughter to the Maharaja of Cooch Behar, who was just fifteen years old at the time. Sen's reasoning was that if the Maharaja could be persuaded to join his association, it would make his influence widespread. These changes alienated many followers, who now founded yet another breakaway society, the *Sadharan Brahmo Samaj*.

As it turned out, the marriage, which was encouraged by the British Administration, proved to be extremely beneficial for the remote state of Cooch Behar. The historian David Knopf says: "In those fourteen years (following his marriage), through increasing the annual revenue of state by 300,000 rupees, the King regularised the administration, established the first railway link to Bengal, improved communication throughout the kingdom with the construction of innumerable roads and bridges, created for the first time a city with a planned sanitation and drainage system, constructed the earliest buildings in the country dedicated to the principles of modern justice and administration, started a large fully equipped hospital in the capital and public dispensaries in the countryside, and founded Cooch Behar's first public library, public parks and gardens, a girls' school, college, and a public marketplace. He also abolished polygamy in the royal family and capital punishment throughout the kingdom". He and his wife also built the largest Brahmo Samaj temple in the country. Sen had certainly known what he was doing, when he married his daughter to the young King!

Sen began to work hard to reinvigorate his own section by a new infusion of Christian ideas and phrases, such as the *New Dispensation*, the *Holy Spirit*, etc. He also instituted a sacramental meal of rice and water, in imitation of the Christian Mass.

Now began a new phase of his life. Two of his famous lectures delivered around this time, reveal his new doctrines. They were *The Marvellous Mystery*, *the Trinity*, and *Asia's Message to Europe*. This last lecture is an eloquent plea against what he calls "the Europeanizing of Asia", as well as a protest against Western sectarianism.

Sen's Brahmo Samaj was against idol or image worship. Their faith was in *saguna nirakara* aspect of God – God without form but with benevolent attributes, as his followers describe it. Many enthusiastic young men, especially bright college students, came under the influence of this liberal sect.

Perhaps this was Sen's greatest contribution to the religion of his ancestors; when he met Sri Ramakrishna

Paramahansa, who was at that time, relatively still unknown, the two were drawn to each other despite wide differences in ideology. Sen and other Brahmos publicized Ramakrishna before the larger public of Bengal through their speeches and writings. Therefore it is said, that "the discovery of Ramakrishna was one of the greatest gifts of the Brahmos to the Bengali intelligentsia of the nineteenth century."

Keshub Chandra Sen passed away in January 1884: he had several bitter critics and enemies; but he had also earned very many warm friends. It is said that Sri Ramakrishna visited him during his last days, and prayed earnestly to the Divine Mother, to spare his brilliant friend. But it was not to be.

Today, we remember Keshub Chandra Sen, for his infusion of *bhakti* into the movement of the Brahmo Samaj. He also found that all the great religious teachers were bound together by a common bond. Next was his faith in the Divine mission of the Brahmo Samaj. Another important contribution was his emphasis of the principle laid down by Ram Mohan Roy – that service of man was the service of God.

Books By Keshub Chandra Sen

- *Lectures in India* by Keshub Chandra Sen
- *The Brahmo Samaj;: The New Dispensation, or the religion of harmony* by Keshub Chandra Sen
- *The New Dispensation* by Keshub Chandra Sen

Books On Keshub Chandra Sen

- *Keshub Chandra Sen And The Brahma Samaj: Being A Brief Review Of Indian Theism From 1830 To 1884 (1884)* by Thomas E. Slater
- *Pilgrimage to Brahmananda Keshub Chandra Sen* by Mati Lal Das
- *Life of Keshub Chander Sen, 1907, Mary Lant Carpenter*
- *Keshub Chandra and Ramkrishna* by Gopal Chandra Banerji
- *Brahmoism, or: History of reformed Hinduism, from its origin in 1830, under Rajah Mohun Roy, to the present time, with a particular account of Babu Keshub Chunder Sen's connection with the movement* by Ram Chandra Bose
- *Ten days with Brahmananda Keshub Chandra Sen (Samanwaya Granthamala series)* by Keshub Chunder Sen

Kanakadasa was a great singer-saint of Karnataka. Born and bred as a warrior and village chieftain, his life was transformed by *bhakti*, and he threw away the sword to take on the *tanpura* and the *tola*, and became a great icon of the *Haridasa* movement which swept across Karnataka in those days. The unique configuration of the sanctum sanctorum in the famous Udipi temple, is a living evidence of his great devotion to the Lord, and the Lord's profound love for him! For in this temple, the deity faces away from the door, and stands today in the same position to which He turned, sideways, to grant *darshan* to this great saint, who was not allowed to enter His temple premises.

Kanakadasa

*O*ver the years, it has been the tradition for us at the Sadhu Vaswani Mission to observe what are called "Hero Days", commemorating the sacred memory of the many great souls who have taken birth in East and West. We believe that these saints have been sent by our Heavenly Father to live amongst us so that we might be drawn towards His grace. Born in different climes and cultures, speaking different languages, using different methods, they have all served as guides and guardians of lost souls, always pointing us towards the light of love, devotion, service and sacrifice, so that we may find our way to the Eternal Home. As I read about them, hear about them and at times, speak to my friends about them, I have been struck by the extraordinary stories of their spiritual growth: believe me, when I say that for many of them, the journey to the Divine has not been easy. They have not trodden a primrose path that took them to God through a short-cut. They did not acquire 'instant *nirvana*' which is promised by some New Age teachers. They followed the steep and thorny path facing numerous obstacles and discouragements. But, I can say with certainty that their struggles were not in vain; for we of the modern age, continue to be inspired by their struggles and their eventual success in attaining the ultimate goal of liberation.

Let me speak to you today of one such great soul, the great singer-saint of Karnataka, who is revered by the name of Kanakadasa. How he came to be known by this name is in itself a fascinating story. According to tradition, Kanakadasa was born the son of a chieftain of the *Kuruba* (shepherd) community who was the *nayaka* (leader) of security forces under a local king. The *kula devata* or the deity worshipped by the family was Adikeshava of Kaginele, which is now only a small village, but at that time, (sixteenth century) a prosperous place and trading center.

The saint I am telling you about, was born in or around 1509, the son of Biregowda and Beechamma. His father was the chief of the village and was also in charge of collecting the interest on the money lent by the king to the local traders. His mother was a devout and religious lady. It is said that God answered their prayers for a child, by blessing them with a male child, whom they named Thimmappa. He became a leader of the youth of the village. All were attracted towards him. The youth idealised him and moved around him. One day, all of a sudden, his father expired. But before passing away, he announced that after him, his son would become the chief of the village. Now Thimmappa took on the job of collecting the interest from the villagers to send to the king.

One day, some of the villagers came to the chief. The village had been reeling under a severe drought for months; the rains had failed for the second successive season. There was an acute shortage of water. Thimmappa came up with the idea of digging a well in the village. They all got together and began to dig the well. All of a sudden, as they dug deeper and deeper underground, they found pots filled with gold! The villagers said spontaneously, "All the gold belongs to our chief Thimmappa, because it was on his instructions that we started digging." In those days it was the custom, that if gold was found under the earth, then it should not be used for personal purposes. Instead, with that gold, a temple should be constructed. Thus, it was that Thimmappa was given all the gold and entrusted with the task of constructing the temple. Thus it was, too, that he acquired the name Kanakadasa.

One of his later compositions describes what seems to be a moving personal experience. From this work we learn that once, Kanakadasa was mortally wounded by enemies, as he was engaged in guarding the King's fortress. He was saved from certain death by the grace of Sri Krishna, who appeared to him in a vision and urged him to surrender himself to the Divine. This was the turning point in the young chieftain's life. He became a disciple of Sant Vyasaraja, and under his Guru's influence, became an ardent Krishna *bhakta*, and a distinguished member of the exclusive group of singing saints known as *Haridasas*, or servants of Sri Hari – i.e. Lord Krishna.

The Haridasa movement ushered in an era of pure and unalloyed *bhakti* in Karnataka. Many were the Haridasa saints who composed songs in praise of Sri Krishna, which are still sung in Karnataka today. From the 15th century to 19th century, we come across several Haridasas who wrote devotional compositions which could be set to music with simple instruments like *Tanpura*, and *Tala* (cymbals). They sang *kirtans*, *bhajans*, and prayers in simple, colloquial Kannada, which had universal appeal among the people, and helped to spread the cult of *bhakti* among the masses. I have already told you about Purandardasa, who was one of the members of this tradition. Kanakadasa too has given us immortal compositions which emphasise the *dvaita* philosophy, and the value of piety, devotion and simplicity.

If Purandardasa gave up his business as a gold trader and exchanged his scales for a *tanpura*, Kanakadasa threw away his sword when the "inner call" came. Purandardasa is supreme among composers. Kanakadasa is a poet among composers. He wrote about two hundred songs (*kirtans, padas* and *mundiges* or philosophical songs), and also composed five major works.

There is a legend that Kanakadasa was asked by his Guru, Vyasaraja, to seek *darshan* of Sri Krishna at the famous Udipi temple. But when he reached Udipi, he was not allowed to enter the shrine by the orthodox Madhwa gurus, as he was not a Brahmin by birth. Kanakadasa accepted this harsh diktat with humility and stationed himself in a corner outside the temple wall. He closed his eyes, and beheld the beauteous form of Sri Krishna which he had been denied the privilege of seeing physically. His inner voice opened and he began singing the praise of Lord Krishna in one beautiful song after another until he was utterly lost to the outside world.

Suddenly there was a breach in the wall, right in front of the spot where Kanaka stood, Lord Krishna offered his full *darshan* to his dear devotee, turning his face towards the poet. Those people who were, at that very moment, privileged to worship before the *sanctum sanctorum* were shocked to see the deity turn sideways, facing away from them. They rushed out to see what was happening. They saw the breach in the wall, and Kanaka standing face to face with his Beloved Lord, in utter ecstasy.

To this day, all devotees who come to offer worship at the famous Udipi temple, first view the Lord's beauteous form through the *Kanakana Kindi* – a small window which was constructed at the breach, in sacred memory of this miraculous incident. The idol of the lovely Bal Krishna at Udipi, even now, does not face the main door of the sanctum sanctorum, but is turned towards Kanaka's window. It is quite another story that the orthodox priests of the temple rushed out to beg

Kanakadasa's forgiveness, and escorted him inside for a special *darshan* of the Lord.

Today that window stands as a tribute to the unique saint of Karnataka. When people strain to have a peep at the idol, through the window, they relive the ecstasy that the saint felt at the divine *darshan*. It is also a memorial to Kanakadasa and eclectic Hindu belief that devotion, song, music, *kirtan* and sainthood transcend all narrow restrictions of caste, creed, birth and conservatism.

Let me end this account of Kanakadasa's inspiring life, with the English translation of one of his memorable songs:

> Are you a creature of illusion? Or, is illusion your creation?
>
> Are you a part of the body? Or, is the body a part of you?
>
> Is space within the house? Or, the house within space?
>
> Or, are both space and the house within the seeing eye?
>
> Is the eye within the mind? Or, the mind within the eye?
>
> Or, are both the eye and the mind within you?
>
> Does sweetness lie in sugar, or sugar in sweetness?
>
> Or, do both sweetness and sugar lie in the tongue?
>
> Is the tongue within the mind? Or, the mind within the tongue?

Or, are both the tongue and the mind within you?
Does fragrance lie in the flower? Or, the flower in fragrance?
Or, do both the flower and fragrance lie in the nostrils?
I cannot say, O Lord Adikeshava of Kaginele,
O, Peerless One, are all things within You alone?

Maharishi Narada

Maharishi Narada is one of the most venerated saints of India. There is hardly a *purana* or scripture in which his name is not mentioned. The ultimate Narayana *bhakta*, Narada drew many souls to the Lord, in the course of his constant wandering across the three worlds. Greatly beloved of Maha Vishnu, Narada was used as an instrument of the Lord's will to participate in many of his *leelas*. Sage Veda Vyasa, Dhruva and Bhakta Prahlada among others, benefited greatly from their association with him.

Maharishi Narada

The great sage Narada is one of the most beloved of the rishis of yore, spoken of in our ancient scriptures. His story is narrated in the *Bhagavata Purana* where we are told that he was the son-disciple of Lord Brahma and was like a Guru to Sage Veda Vyasa. I would like to frame the remarkable portrait of this *maharishi*, by placing it as 'a story within a story'.

The Katha Upanishad begins with this memorable story. A poor Brahmin called Vajasravas once decided to perform a *yagna*. This was no ordinary *yagna*; it was the 'Vishwajeet *yagna*', for which it is stipulated that a man must donate all his wealth, all his possessions, in return for assurance of heaven.

Now, the poor Brahmin was not rich in the wealth of this world, and the 'treasures' that he offered in the *yagna* were just a few very old cows, and a few battered vessels. That was all he had, and that was all he could offer to those participating in the *yagna*.

The poor Brahmin had a very intelligent son, called Nachiketa. The young lad watched his father's 'treasures' being given away and he was both saddened and puzzled. He thought to himself, "What kind of heaven will my father attain, by giving away cows that cannot even move, leave alone calve or give milk?" His concern for his father was genuine; he knew that in a *yagna,* a man had to offer the best that he had. His father had a son – himself, Nachiketa, who was sound of mind and body, and pious and intelligent as well. "What is my father doing, keeping me back, and offering worthless gifts as offerings? If the *yagna* is to achieve its purpose, he must surely give me away, for a son is a man's richest treasure. It is better that my father gives me away as an offering. I am his dear beloved child. If he gives me away, then this *yagna* will truly be blessed."

Without further ado, the boy marched up to his father who was giving away the 'gifts' and demanded of him, "Father, have you given me away yet?"

That was his ploy to remind his father that his son was ready to be given away, to ensure the success of the *yagna.* The father, who certainly had not interpreted the injunction to give away his wealth so seriously, just ignored the boy and his cheeky question.

But Nachiketa was not being cheeky. He loved his father, and he venerated the scriptures and the rules of the sacred *yagnas.* So he repeated his question, "Father, am I not your treasure, your most valuable possession? Have you given me away to someone?"

When this embarrassing question was repeated a third time, the father lost his patience and shouted, "Yes, I have! I have given you away to the Lord of Death!"

Nachiketa was certainly taken aback: but it was an abstract issue which haunted him. "Some people rate me among the best of the youth; others think I am no more than average; what could my father gain by offering me to the Lord of Death?"

The boy realised that his father had spoken in anger; but the words had been uttered; and their promise had to be fulfilled. Nachiketa decided then and there, that he would offer himself to Yama, the god of Death, as his father had said.

It is said that Nachiketa comforted his distraught father, and travelled alone to the bounds of the world, to reach the abode of the Lord of Death. Not finding Yama at home, the boy waited for three days and three nights to meet him. Three days and three nights the boy sat patiently, without food, without water, without a wink of sleep!

When Yama returned home, he was amazed to see the young boy waiting outside his gates. Here was an *atithi*, a guest at his door, a youngster who had been left unattended, with no courtesy extended to him, no hospitality shown, not so much as a drink of water offered to him, leave alone food to eat! Our scriptures enjoin us to treat visitors like gods: *atithi devo bhava!* Yama felt it was a grievous offence that had been committed, although it had been inadvertent, unintentional on his part.

He approached the boy with great affection and regard and said to him, "O, young brahmin! You have lived in my abode for three days and three nights without food, water and sleep! Allow me to make up for this lapse by offering to you three boons — one for each day you have been kept waiting."

Let me invite you to guess: what do you think the young boy asked for? I wonder what we would have asked for, if we were in his place!

First and foremost, Nachiketa's thoughts move out to his father. He knew that his father had sent him here in anger. "May my father be saved from anger," the boy thinks. Aloud, he tells Yamaraja, "O, Lord, so bless my father that he may be freed from the disease of anger. When I happen to meet him or when he chances to meet me, may I find him free from anxiety and anger, in calmness of mind, and reconciled to me in every respect."

Yama is well pleased with the filial piety of the boy, and says to him, "So be it! Whatever you wish will happen. Seeing you freed from the jaws of death, all traces of anger will disappear from your father's heart. Reunited with his son, he will indeed be restored to peace and joy. His love and affection for you will revive, as before."

What is the second boon which Nachiketa seeks? First and foremost, he had been concerned about his father. His second thought moves out to this sad, sad world. "There is so much suffering upon earth," he thinks. "But there is so much happiness in the heaven world. They are not troubled by hunger or thirst here. They never fall sick, they never grow old. They are all so happy here. How can people be taught to free themselves from the sorrow and suffering of the world, and find their way to Heaven?"

And so Nachiketa tells Yamaraja, "The second boon I ask of you is this: kindly show us the path, that path which the people can take that will lead them to happiness and then to the heaven world."

Yamaraja is, again, well pleased with the boy's selfless desire to help others. He replies, "My dear one, this is not a big issue at all. I will tell you about a *yagna*, which if anyone performs, he will definitely reach the heaven world. Suffering will not touch him; he will experience all joy and happiness in the heaven world. You are so young and yet you are filled with the spirit of humane compassion, that I shall name this *yagna* after you – from now on, it will be called Nachiketa *Yagna*." And Yamaraja proceeds to explain the *yagna*, promising that whosoever performs the *yagna* with faith and piety, would attain heaven.

What is the third boon he asks for? This young child says to his mentor and kind benefactor, the

Lord of Death, "I know for sure, that many people attain to the heaven world, but they all come back. They come back into this cycle of birth and death. O, how they are crushed in this ever revolving wheel! Pray, teach me how they may be freed from this terrible, crushing burden!"

Does not Sant Kabir say to us:

Chalti Chakki Dekh Kar, diya Kabira Roi,
Do Paatan ke Beech Mein, Saabhit Raya Na Koi.

Between the two slabs of the grinding stone,
Everything gets crushed.
Seeing this Kabira laments,
That nothing survives the wheel of life!

Yamaraja is amazed at the boy's wisdom and his determined quest to seek the ultimate Truth about life and the goal of life: Liberation. He tells the boy, "You have asked a very difficult question. Even the *devtas* do not know of this way. Even the gods have quarreled over the issue. It is abstruse and complex, and you are very young. Ask for something else instead, and I will happily grant it to you. Land, cows, horses, elephants, gold, silver, the kingdoms of the earth, whatever you ask I shall give you – ask for wealth and a long life, sons and grandsons. It will all be granted to you. Beautiful girls will be in your service, who will sing songs for you, and fill your life with pleasure. I will give you everything, but do not ask me to give you an answer to this question."

Nachiketa tells him, "I could of course ask you for land, cows, elephants, all the pleasures and the wealth of this world – but Lord, you know and I know, these are ephemeral, they are but passing pleasures. They may be mine today, but gone tomorrow. How can I call them mine? I seek from you that treasure, the treasure of truth, which is truly lasting; and who better than You, the Lord of Death, to give me the right answer to this question? Show me the path to true and absolute freedom, tell me, how one may know his true self, because I know he will not be able to attain God, unless he attains self-realisation. His senses, his knowledge are of no avail to him in this quest for truth. Therefore, Lord, I seek nothing else from You, but this sacred truth."

Yamraja sees that this boy has faith; he has sincerity; he has purity; he has tenacity of purpose, he is free from temptation and above all he has that deep inner longing to know the truth and realise it in his own right. The Lord of Death realises that if anyone is entitled to know the sacred truth, it is this young Brahmin lad.

And thus begins one of the most memorable discourses recorded in the Upanishads – the two paths of *shreya* and *preya*, the preferable and the pleasurable. Yamaraja tells Nachiketa the path to God realisation is the path of *shreya*. Neither the senses nor the mind can help us to attain this path, for they only pull us outwards, to the external world. If we want to attain God, we must go within, within the temple of the heart, where the Lord Himself is seated. Only the one who goes within, attains God while the one who runs outwards moves further and further away from God.

It is the way of meditation. Sitting in silence, he opens one veil after another. There are so many veils. These veils hide the light that shines inside everyone of us. He draws closer and closer to the living light within. Hence, this is the way of self control. It is the way of self-knowledge, self-annihilation, service and sacrifice.

Yamraja tells Nachiketa, "My dear one, above the senses is the mind and above the mind is the *buddhi* – the power of understanding, the power of discrimination. Above the *buddhi* is the *Aatman*, but over and above the *Aatman* is the *Paramatma*. Even above the *Parmatama* is the unmanifest *adrishta*. But above it all is the *Para Brahma* – who transcends both the manifest and the unmanifest, because He synthesises both of them inside."

Yamaraja tells Nachiketa that when all desires die within the mind and when all doubts are dispelled, then verily does man attain to the Supreme.

In the end Yamraja tells Nachiketa, "My child, this path, which I have told you today – it is a narrow path, a difficult and slippery one. As you walk on this path, you will have to face so many trials and tribulations, and a time will come when you will feel you are walking on the edge of a razor. You will have to face all these difficulties. But if you persist in your efforts unflinchingly, and continue on this path with faith and piety, you will attain to the Supreme."

Many are the difficulties which a pilgrim has to face on the path of *shreya*. These multifarious difficulties are well illustrated for our benefit and learning in the life of Maharishi Narada, one of the greatest sages mentioned in many of our ancient scriptures such as the Vedas, the Upanishads, the Bhagavad Gita, the Ramayana, the Mahabharata, and several other *Puranas*.

Who was Narada? Narada was called a Maharishi, he was a divine sage. According to legends, he is regarded as the *Manasaputra* in reference to his birth 'from the mind of Brahma'. According to this legend, he was the first living being as described in the Puranic universe. This was his unique mark — he had the name of Sri Narayana constantly on his lips and in the heart within. Narada sang the name of God at all times, "*Bhajmann Narayan, Bhajmann Narayan*". This is why Narada Muni is very dear to the Vaishnava traditions. In the Puranic scriptures, he is listed as one of the twelve mahajanas, or 'great devotees' of Lord Vishnu. With this name on his lips, Narada moved from one place to another, looking into the condition of the people, concerned at all times with their well being.

Tulsidas mentions that the path of the pilgrim is full of difficulties. The pilgrim cannot even sleep for a minute. He has to be awake all the time. In the Nuri Granth, Gurudev Sadhu Vaswani urges us repeatedly:

"Uth jaag chowkidar, uth jaag chowkidar!" Arise, Awake O, Watchman! For that must be the motto of the life of every seeker after truth! He has to keep awake all the twenty four hours, because the minute he falls asleep, the 'thieves' are ready, they come and steal his spiritual treasure. He has to be awake all the while.

Tulsidas tells us that it was Narada who imparted this teaching to the four sons of Prajapati, who came to sit at the lotus feet of the sage. They said to Narada, "You are the divine sage, we pray that you may teach us." Narada teaches these four children. They are young, their hearts are unstained. When Narada teaches them, the spirit of detachment arises within them; the feeling of sacrifice enters within them. All four become determined that they will not enter the cycle of *sansara*. They resolve to become *tapasvis*.

When Prajapati hears of this, he is very angry. He is very upset that Narada has made all his four sons into *tyagis, sanyasis*. If Narada turns all other youngsters into *Tyagis* and *Sanyasis*, then how will God's creation multiply? The reason for which Prajapati was created in the first place was only to ensure that creation multiplies. This purpose has been utterly defeated by Narada's teaching!

In anger Prajapati curses Narada. He says, "I curse you Narada – you will not stay for long in any one place. You will keep moving from one place to another. If you are permitted to dwell in any one place, then one or other youngster may be drawn to you and your teachings, and end up as *Vairagis* and *Sanyasis*. Hence, I curse you."

Thus it was that Maharishi Narada became a *triloka sanchari* – one who wanders across the three worlds. That is why we see Narada, as the one who keeps on moving from one place to another, with a *veena* in his hands and with the Name of God on his lips. To all devotees of the Lord, he extends his helping hand. Wherever he goes, he keeps on glorifying the Name of the Lord, urging devotion to the Lotus feet of the Lord. His remarkable work, the *Narada Bhakti Sutras* capture the very essence of the spirit of devotion to the Lord. These *sutras* or brilliant aphorisms are said to constitute a veritable manual of *bhakti yoga*.

There is yet another story told to us in the Bhagavata Purana of Narada's initiation as a great sage and *tapasvi*. It is said that he was a *gandharva* or divine being, who was cursed to be born on this earth. He took birth as the son of a humble maidservant, who earned her living in the service of a devout Brahmin. The Brahmin and his wife were so pleased with her devotion to duty that they shared with her, the *prasad* of their daily *pooja* to Lord Vishnu. It is also said that having partaken of this *prasad*, Narada was imbued with overwhelming devotion to Lord Vishnu. When his mother died, he decided to seek the *tapovan*, to meditate on the Lord and attain to his lotus feet. So devout and so dedicated was he at his austerities, that Lord Vishnu appeared before him, and granted him the boon that he would ultimately become a divine being; the vision that had been granted to him in this birth was only to fill him with piety and inspiration to attain to a higher life through death. Thus was the sacred soul of Narada granted liberation by the Lord's grace. At the end of that cycle or *yuga*, when the *pralaya* (floods) came to end the created world, Narada was reborn – this time, as the *manasaputra* of Brahma, through the divine sanction of Lord Vishnu. He had been freed from all material attachments, and granted an ethereal form free of the taints of the senses. He could now travel everywhere without restriction, both in the heavenly world and in the material world.

Many are the stories that have come to us of this great sage and his *triloka sanchara*. Let me share a few with you.

A long time ago, before you and I were born, and when the world was a much better place, there was a simple farmer living happily in a small village. This farmer used to work hard for his living, tilling his crops from morn to night. He took simple pride in his work and was never happier than when he was in his field. The farmer believed devoutly in God and prayed to Him three times a day: Once, before starting his work, the second time before having his lunch, and the third time before going to bed.

One day, Narada approached Lord Vishnu and asked him: "Lord, You have so many followers all over the world. But tell me, among all of them, who is Your favourite devotee?" Vishnu smiled and answered, "I love all My devotees, but yes, there is a farmer in a small village whom I love and admire more than the others."

Hearing this, Narada, being extremely curious, set out at once to find out why this farmer was Lord Vishnu's favourite. Now, it so happened that this farmer was the same one we were talking about in the beginning of the story. Narada observed the farmer from high up in the heavens for a few weeks, and then returned to Vishnu, very confused. He confronted Vishnu with his questions. 'Lord," he said, "I have observed the farmer, and I am very disappointed. He only takes Your Name three times a day, and the rest of his time he devotes to working in his field and taking care of his family. He has done nothing extraordinary. Why then is he Your favourite devotee, instead of the many sages who have devoted their entire lives to meditating on Your greatness?"

Lord Vishnu smiled and then said, "Narada, the answer to this question lies in a task I am going to set for you. You must carry this pot, full of oil, on your head and go around the world."

Narada started laughing on hearing this easy task. "But, let Me warn you," continued Lord Vishnu, "not a single drop must spill from the pot, otherwise, you have failed in your quest." Narada agreed, and balancing on his head the pot which was filled to the brim with oil, he began his journey around the world.

In the beginning, Narada was convinced it was a very easy task, but very soon, he found out how wrong he had been. It required utmost concentration to balance the pot on his head and ensure that not a single drop spilled from it. Carefully and slowly, step by step, Narada finally completed this difficult task and approached Vishnu, tired and worn out.

However, he was still wondering why the farmer was Lord Vishnu's favourite. Lord Vishnu greeted him warmly and congratulated him on completing the task successfully. He then asked Narada, "Tell me, Narada, when you were balancing the pot on your head and going around the world, how many times did you take My Name or think of Me?"

Narada was taken aback at the question and stammered, "But Lord... I did not have the time to think of You... I was so busy concentrating on the pot of oil. How can You expect me to carry out Your task and think of You at the same time? It is impossible!"

Lord Vishnu then answered gravely, "Narada, the farmer, who is my best devotee, is also carrying out a difficult task, that of tending to his crops and caring for his family. It is a task that I have assigned to him, which takes up all his time. Yet, he still finds the time to think of Me and pray to Me, not just once, but THREE TIMES a day. You, who take My name every day, could not find the time to think of Me when you were carrying out your task. This is the difference between all the others and the farmer. I love all My children, but I love them all the more when they do their work uncomplainingly, are good to others and think of Me at least once during the day. That is all I ask of them."

Narada then begged forgiveness, and after thanking the Lord, went away, much enlightened.

Once, Rishi Narada approached Lord Vishnu and requested him humbly: "My Lord! Do tell me about the value and influence of *satsang*. I am eager to know what it can do for the seeker."

Lord Vishnu smiled at Narada. He said, "I am so busy now, I do not have the time to talk to you about it. But I would like to help you. Please go to the giant banyan tree in the forest located at the foot of the Meru Hills. There you will find a squirrel. He will enlighten you about *satsang*."

Rishi Narada was puzzled. A squirrel — to enlighten him on *satsang!* But the Lord's word was absolute, and Narada did as he was told. He found the tree in question, and a lively squirrel jumped down before him.

In all respect, Narada said to him, "I pray you, dear squirrel, enlighten me on the value and influence of *satsang*."

The squirrel looked at Narada with its beady, bright eyes for what seemed to be a long drawn out minute. Narada looked into its eyes and held his gaze. At the end of the minute the squirrel curled up, lifeless. It was dead!

Taken aback, Narada found his way back to *Vaikunth,* where he narrated the moving incident to the Lord. "I hope I have not been instrumental in the death of the poor creature," he lamented. "And, dear Lord, my question is still unanswered. Wilt Thou enlighten me?"

"I'm afraid that's not possible Narada," replied the Lord. "Go back to the same tree. You will find a monkey, who will give you the knowledge you seek."

Faithfully, Narada did as he was told. Indeed, he found the monkey swinging from one branch to another. When he saw Narada, the monkey jumped down with a thud.

"I pray you, O monkey, to enlighten me on the value of *satsang,*" Narada said to the monkey respectfully.

The monkey drew close and looked deep into Narada's eyes. In a minute, he dropped dead at the sage's feet.

This time, Narada was nonplussed. In utter shock, he rushed to Lord Vishnu and said: "Lord, I do not know what is wrong. The monkey You mentioned has also dropped dead before my eyes. What am I doing to these poor creatures? Who will now enlighten me on the *satsang?*"

"Well, Narada," said Lord Vishnu. "Tomorrow a prince will be born in the royal family of the kingdom in which the forest is located. Go and bless the new born child – and he will enlighten you on the matter you seek."

"But... my Lord..." stammered Narada. "When I consider the fate of the squirrel... and the monkey... how can I dare to approach this innocent, newborn baby?"

"Do you or don't you need enlightenment on *satsang?*" asked the Lord with a smile. "Go to the child. Your quest will be fulfilled."

It was with a trembling heart that Narada entered the royal palace the next morning. The King and Queen were deeply honoured to see him. They welcomed him with all ceremony that was due to a *maharishi*. They entreated him to bless their newborn son – the heir to the throne.

Rishi Narada was taken to the room where the baby prince lay asleep in the cradle. His heart beat fast as he laid his hand on the brow of the child to bless him.

No sooner had he touched the child, than the baby opened its eyes and looked deep into the eyes of the Rishi.

"O Prince," said Rishi Narada, a cold sweat breaking out over his forehead. "Lord Vishnu bade me come to you to ask you about the value of the *satsang*."

To the Rishi's utter amazement, the baby began to speak. "Rishi Narada, you see me here – the manifest proof of the value of *satsang*. In my previous births, I was a squirrel, and then a monkey. As a squirrel, I was only motivated by appetite. I did nothing but gather and hoard. When I met you and looked into your eyes, I was released from that birth. My *karma* caused me to take birth as a monkey. Then again, I had the good fortune to encounter you at close quarters. Released from that incarnation, I have risen in the scale of evolution to take birth as a Prince in the pious family of the King of this country. If one minute in the company of a holy one like you could help me this far, I leave you to judge what the value and influence of sustained *satsang* can be!"

Rishi Narada was overjoyed. The Lord had indeed performed a *leela* to teach His humble devotee the value of *satsang*.

Indeed, many were the *leelas* that the Lord performed. Once, the sage went on one of his many pilgrimages. One night, he received the hospitality of a poor, childless couple, who served him with deep love and piety. In the morning, when Narada was about to depart, the householder humbly begged him, "You are beloved of Lord Vishnu. O, please tell Him to bless us with a child."

Narada was so moved by the request that he made a beeline to Vaikunth, where he met Lord Vishnu. "Dear Lord, be merciful to this humble devotee of yours. Bless that man with a child," implored the sage.

"I am sorry," said the Lord. "It is not in the destiny of that man to have a child."

Narada went on his way, disappointed.

Five years later, happening to pass the same way, he was once again received by the hospitable couple. To his amazement, he saw not one, but two children playing at the door of the hut.

"Whose children are these?" he asked in disbelief.

"Ours," said the man. "Soon after you left us last time, our prayers were answered. My wife and I have been truly blessed."

Narada hastened to confront Lord Vishnu. "How could You be so mistaken?" he shouted. "You said it was not in the destiny of that man to have children! Now he has two of them!"

The Lord laughed aloud. "That must be the doing of a saint," he said. "Surely you know Narada, association with a saint has the power to change destiny!"

Maharishi Narada once said to Sri Krishna that he wanted to experience the power of *Vishnu maya*.

"So be it," answered the Lord, "but not now."

Years passed. One day, Sri Krishna sat on a secluded mountain slope with his beloved devotee, Narada Muni.

As they talked, Sri Krishna became thirsty. He asked Narada to bring some water.

Promptly, Narada Muni set out to fetch water for his beloved Lord. He looked, here, there, everywhere. Not a drop of water was to be found. Narada's anxiety grew every minute. His beloved Sri Krishna was thirsty! It was imperative that he should take water to quench his Lord's thirst and soon!

At a distance, he saw a cottage. Walking up to it hastily, he knocked at the door. Surely, he thought, the lady of the house would spare him a bowl of water to take to Sri Krishna. The door was opened, and Narada saw before him, the most beautiful woman that his eyes had ever beheld! Verily, she was like an *apsara*, descended from the skies.

Lord Krishna was forgotten; the water was forgotten, as Narada's gaze became transfixed upon the beauteous form before him.

"You have captivated me utterly," he said to the woman. "I beg you to marry me and be my wife!"

And so it came to pass that they were married. Narada Muni revelled in the pleasures of a worldly married life. Soon they begot children, and his bonds tied him down to the world even more firmly.

Such is the power of *maya* – worldly illusion – that we are enticed by worldly appearances and manifestations, and forget our Divine selves and God, our Creator. The great sage, Narada, was no exception.

In the course of time, the village in which they lived was struck by an epidemic. Narada left the village with his family in search of a safe place to live. On the way, they had to cross a river in spate. Halfway across the river, a powerful current swept away his wife and children. Narada began to weep in anguish and sorrow.

Just then he heard a voice, "I am thirsty, Narada, won't you bring me a cup of water?"

With a shock, Narada recognised the familiar voice! It was none other than the voice of Sri Krishna, who had asked him to fetch water.

Narada repented deeply, awakening from the *maya* that had held him in thrall so long. Had not he set out to fetch water to quench the Lord's thirst? How deeply the allure of *maya* had trapped him, that he had even forgotten his dearly beloved Sri Krishna! Truly, he said to himself, tremendous is the power of *maya*.

Sage Narada had the ability to bring about a remarkable spiritual change in everyone with whom he came into contact. Loved as a favourite *bhakta* of the *trimurtis* and their *devis*, he did everything he could to draw people closer to God. It was he who turned the dacoit Ratnakar into Sage Valmiki; it was he who instilled the love of Sriman Narayana in the heart of Prahlada, while the latter was still in his mother's womb. It was again Narada, who gave Druva his sacred mantra: *Om Namo Bhagavate Vasudevaya!*

Blessed be his name!

Sayings of Narada

Devotional service manifests as the most elevated, pure love for God.

* * * * *

The renunciation, indeed, is in the total giving up of all secular and religious activities.

* * * * *

The supreme devotion (*bhakti*) is indeed, as a technique even superior to the path of action (*karma*), the path of knowledge (*gyana*), and the path of disciplined contemplation (*yoga*).

* * * * *

Indeed the sources of devotion are explored and exploited fully through renunciation of sense-objects and also by giving up attachments to being around.

* * * * *

Primarily it (pure devotion) is gained through the grace of great souls, or through a little of the divine grace.

* * * * *

To come in contact with a great soul is indeed extremely difficult. It is impossible to know them fully. Yet, it is infallible in its effect.

* * * * *

Who crosses *maya* (illusion)? Who really crosses maya? He who gives up all attachments to sense-objects: He who serves the great devotees and he who renounces all sense of possession in himself. He who keeps himself in a solitary place of quietude, he who plucks off his bondage with the world by the roots, (he who) goes beyond the influences of his "*gunas*", (he who) renounces all his anxieties for acquiring and maintaining. He who relinquishes the fruits of actions, who renounces all ego-centric actions, and thus becomes free from the play of the pairs of opposites. He who renounces even the Vedas and gains a pure unbroken flow of devotion. He crosses, indeed he crosses. He helps others also to cross.

Books By Narada

- *Narada Bhakti Sutras*

Books On Narada

- *The Bhagavata Purana*
- *The Nâradasmriti – Translation* by Richard W. Lariviere
- *Narada's Way of Divine Love* by Swami Prabhavananda
- *The Yoga of Spiritual Devotion: A Modern Translation of the Narada Bhakti Sutras* by Prem Prakash
- *Narada Bhakti Sutras - The Aphorisms of Love* by Sri Sri Ravishankar and Sharmala Murarka
- *Ancient Indian Tradition & Mythology: Volume 18 Narada PURANA PART IV* by J. L. (editor) Shastri
- *Narada Bhakti Sutras: Aphorisms on The Gospel of Divine Love [with Sanskrit text, word-by-word meaning, English rendering of the text and elaborate explanatory and critical Notes]* by Swami Tyagisananda
- *Ancient Indian Tradition and Mythology: Mahapuranas -The Narada Purana* by Unesco
- *Tales of Narada (Amar Chitra Katha)* by Anant Pai

St. Monica

St. Monica was a devoted Catholic, a sweet and sensitive woman, and a mother who fought a brave, lifelong battle to save the soul of her son from the ways of evil. In intellectual, material and emotional terms, her beloved son Augustine had grown remote from her and his faith. It was the remarkable achievement of her life, that her prayers, exhortations and intense devotion reclaimed her son for the church. Today, we cannot speak of St. Augustine without our heartfelt tribute to his saintly mother.

St. Monica

I would like to tell you about a saint of the Catholic church, who was not only a pure devotee of Jesus Christ, but also a faithful and dutiful wife, and a dedicated mother. We have heard of many saints who turned their back on worldly life, to devote their all to the Lord. Monica was a woman who spent most of her life caring for her husband and children. And yet, she is venerated today as the patron saint of the church, as the one who offers special support and succour to those who have difficult marriages, disappointing children, women who are victims of adultery or unfaithfulness, and wives who are victims of physical and verbal abuse.

The faithful flock of the church know Monica as the mother of one of the foremost saints of the church, St. Augustine. In fact, much of what we know of her, comes to us from *The Confessions of St. Augustine*. With what love and reverence, with what shame and regret does Augustine write of his mother, who was almost singlehandedly responsible for his rehabilitation and return to the Faith of Catholicism! He writes extensively of his dear mother and her life, and these are among the most moving tributes ever paid to a mother by a son!

Monica was of Berber descent, and born in Roman occupied Africa, in an affluent family of early Christians. She is thought to have been born in the year 332 A.D., when many people in the Roman Empire had yet to accept Christianity. So much so, Monica was given away in marriage to a non-Christian (Pagan, as they were called in those days). Her husband was Patricius, a Roman government official posted at Thagaste in what we now call Algeria, and was part of Roman North Africa.

What can I tell you of Patricius? Not a lot that is good, I am afraid! He was a violent and abusive man, given to illicit relationships with women outside the sacred bonds of marriage. Not being a Christian himself, he did not offer any support to his wife in her spiritual aspirations. His mother was also a hot tempered and cruel woman. Many were the trials and tribulations that young Monica was subjected to in the early years of her married life.

A young girl enters the married state with hopes and dreams of a peaceful, harmonious life, a convivial domestic environment, love and loyalty from her husband, affection and support from her mother-in-law, and respect and obedience from her children. Are not these the best gifts of marriage? Is not a woman entitled to these gifts in return for leaving her family and entering the home of strangers to become one among them? Alas, Monica was denied these simple pleasures. Her husband often subjected her to violent abuse, and her mother-in-law only made her life more miserable.

What did Monica do? Did she complain loudly? Did she become bitter and frustrated? Did she walk out of her marriage and return to her affluent father? No! She stayed on with her husband. She bore the abuse and ill-treatment that was meted out to her patiently. That was not all; she returned nothing but love and kindness to her 'tormentors'. What is more, when other women came to her with their problems, she counselled them patiently and taught them to return love and kindness for abuse and pain. In fact, even in her lifetime, she became an apostle of help and support to battered wives. So much so, we are told that her husband Patricius, hardly ever used physical violence against her; and in course of time, he came to appreciate the virtues of the saintly woman he had married. In later years, under his wife's influence, he actually embraced the Christian faith.

I wonder how many of my readers will really appreciate Monica's virtue, her patience, her forbearance and her almost limitless capacity to bear suffering and abuse! Today, there are still many women like her, trapped in unhappy, abusive marriages, unable to escape, unable to seek help from any source. The one source of support that

Monica had is still available to them — and that is strong, firm, unshakable faith in the Lord, and the courage to accept all that comes to them with fortitude. But how many of us are capable of such faith?

Monica was a woman of tremendous faith. The Lord gave her hope, courage and patience to return love for hatred. She never ever gave up hope. She never ever despaired of her wayward husband. And her patience was not in vain. She and Patricius had three children, Navigius, who seems to have been an exemplary son, Augustine, who, as we all know led a notoriously wayward life but was converted to the faith of his mother miraculously, and Perpetua, a daughter, who became a nun. We can say that Monica's influence on her children was the force behind their lives. Patricius too, was a good father to his children, and did everything he could to provide them with the best education.

Here is what St. Augustine says about this difficult period of his mother's life:

"...Her patience was so great that even her husband's infidelity never became a cause of quarreling between them... she never ceased to try to gain him for Thee (Jesus Christ) as a convert, for the virtues with which Thou hadst adorned her, and for which he respected, loved, and admired her, were like so many voices constantly speaking to him of Thee..."

Those voices spoke to her difficult mother-in-law as well, for her son tells us that "she won the older woman over by her dutiful attentions and her constant patience and gentleness – and the two women lived together in wonderful harmony and mutual goodwill." Ultimately both pagan husband and pagan mother-in-law were converted as a result of St. Monica's good example.

Neighbours as well as family benefitted from her virtues. "Whenever she could," writes her son, "she used to act the part of the peacemaker between souls in conflict over some quarrel," never tale-bearing "except for such things as were likely to reconcile them," she did her best, he continues, "to put an end to their quarrels by kind words. This was my mother's way, learned in the school of her heart, where Thou wast her secret teacher."

Augustine was easily the most intelligent and gifted among the three children. His father decided to send him to Carthage, a centre of learning in those days, so that he might develop his talents and become a man of culture. Alas, this proved to be the young man's undoing. He took to learning naturally, and excelled in his studies, especially philosophy; but being sent away from home had a detrimental effect on his character; he took to wild and licentious ways and spent much of his time in philandering and carousing. Monica had tried her best to bring him up as a Christian, but in Carthage, he came under the influence of the Manicheans, and decided to embrace their sect.

According to experts, Manichaeism is a religion founded by the Persian Mani in the latter half of the third century. It claimed to be the true synthesis of all the religious systems then known, and actually incorporated elements of Zoroastrian Dualism, Babylonian folklore, Buddhist ethics, and also some small and superficial aspects of Christianity. Manichaeism professed to be a religion of pure reason as opposed to Christian faith and belief; it professed to explain the origin, the composition, and even the future of the universe; it had an answer for everything! Above all, it despised Christianity, which was beginning to take root in those days. It spread with extraordinary rapidity in its early years, and many young men like Augustine were drawn to it in those times.

Here is what the Catholic Encyclopedia tells us of this period of his life:

When he reached Carthage, towards the end of the year 370 A.D., every circumstance tended to draw him from his true course: the many seductions of the great city that was still half pagan, the licentiousness of other students, the theatres, the intoxication of his literary success, and a proud desire always to be first, even in evil.

When he returned home after his initial stint at Carthage, Monica was shocked to see him changed for the worse. Imagine her horror, when her son told her of his liaison with a woman who had actually borne him a son outside marriage! Monica was deeply grieved.

But she had already learnt that the best way to conquer adversity and suffering was through faith. Her husband Patricius, who had caused a lot of unhappiness to her in their early married life, came to appreciate her virtue, and in the year 371 A.D., on his deathbed, he actually embraced Christianity in deference to her wishes. Her other children gave her no cause for concern. And so, from now on, she had only one aim, one goal in life: a single minded effort to draw her beloved Augustine back to the path of virtue, and to the faith of Christianity.

It would take her the rest of her life to accomplish this purpose!

Augustine's faith and his morals had both been corrupted by his licentious lifestyle and the company he kept at Carthage. In vain did Monica implore him to give up on his sinful life; in vain did she weep, fast and pray for his reformation. The path of evil is not easy to leave.

Perhaps Augustine's innate intelligence and his inborn curiosity worked against him. He himself tells us that he was greatly attracted by the "free philosophy" of Manichaeism, which was unrestrained by faith or dogma; by the boasts of the Manichaens, who claimed that they had discovered contradictions in the Bible; and, above all, by the hope of finding in their doctrine a 'scientific' explanation of nature and the universe. Perhaps the most attractive aspect of the sect was the complete moral irresponsibility enjoyed by its followers. Is this not enough to corrupt a young and ardent soul with intellectual bent?

Augustine had by now completed his studies. He returned to Tagaste to become a teacher of rhetoric. He was strong-willed, stubborn, and not infrequently deceitful with his mother. So powerful was his influence, so eloquent were his persuasive powers that his pupils and even some of his father's friends, converted to Manichaeism, including a kind patron who had lent money to his father to send Augustine to Carthage!

Monica was in deep despair. As a mother, she felt she should not take a lenient view of her son's conduct and attitude. In fact, at one point, she seriously considered asking Augustine to leave the family home. But a saintly priest who was her confessor, advised her against this move. He said to her, "The son of so many tears cannot perish!" This gave her the courage to persist in her prayers, hoping against hope that her dear son would be reformed one day.

Augustine, in the meanwhile, continued to grow in intellectual stature. He won a coveted prize at a Poetry Tournament, and became widely acclaimed as a scholar and philosopher. Many of his noted treatises including a famous work on Aesthetics were written around this time.

Seeking wider horizons to display his talents, Augustine decided to travel to Italy in 383 A.D. Knowing that his mother would not consent to this plan, he left home under subterfuge, without informing her. What did Monica do? She followed him to Italy! She firmly believed that he needed her proximity, her benign influence and, above all, her prayers. In Milan, she actually succeeded in getting him to break off his fifteen year old association with his concubine. But Augustine's ordeals were not at an end. He had to pass through three more years of passion and search. He acquired another concubine, driving his mother to despair yet again. But this time, the aberration was short lived. Under the influence of the Bishop of Milan, Ambrose, the wayward son of this saintly mother, turned at long last, to his mother's faith. He was baptized by Bishop Ambrose at Milan, on Easter day, 387 A.D. Seventeen long years of tears and prayers had his mother spent in single minded pursuit of his eventual reform! She reaped the reward of her faith when she finally saw her son baptized by the Rev. Father who would also become St. Ambrose.

In the autumn of the same year, Monica was called to her heavenly abode.

A moving anecdote is narrated about her last wish. Friends told Augustine that she would not grieve over dying and being buried in a foreign land, for she had added, with a touch of humour, that she was sure God would remember where she was buried and raise her up. She had previously told Augustine and his brother Navigius: "Lay this body anywhere, and take no trouble over it. One thing only do I ask of you, that you remember me at the altar of the Lord wherever you may be." Such absolute faith in God's mercy and grace was a characteristic virtue of this great lady. St. Monica's remains are venerated in the church of St. Augustine, Rome, Italy.

Both pious Christians and avid readers will tell you, that there are no pages of greater pathos and sentiment than the story of her saintly death and Augustine's grief at her loss, than the account given in his autobiography, *The Confessions of St. Augustine*: the work outlines Augustine's sinful youth and his conversion to Christianity under the influence of his mother. It is one of the most powerful and moving works in all literature.

In repeated references to her anguish and the incessant tears and prayers which she poured forth for his conversion during the long years when he went astray, St. Monica's great son waxes most eloquent: "Night and day my mother poured out her tears to Thee and offered her heart-blood in sacrifice for me ...Thou didst rescue my soul from the depths of this darkness because my mother, Thy faithful servant, wept to Thee for me, shedding more tears for my spiritual death than other mothers shed for the bodily death of a son."

"My son," she said to him shortly before her death, "for my part I find no further pleasure in this life. What I am still to do or why I am here in the world, I do not know, for I have no more to hope for on this earth. There was one reason, and one alone, why I wished to remain a little longer in this life, and that was to see you a Catholic Christian before I died. God has granted my wish and more besides, for I now see you as His servant, spurning such happiness as the world can give. What is left for me to do in this world?'

When St. Augustine, became the Bishop of Hippo in Roman Africa, he wrote his *Confessions*. That was ten years later, and in this inspiring work, he could not too highly praise the saintly mother whose tears and prayers had saved him from hell. To him she was the epitome of Catholic womanhood. Accounts of her pious activities and praise for her endearing virtues pervade the work. He pays tribute to "the contrite and humble heart of that chaste and gentle widow, so ready to give alms, so full of humble reverence for Thy saints, who never let a day go by unless she had brought an offering to Thy altar, and never failed to come to Thy church twice every day, each morning and night." He expresses his admiration of her wise and edifying conversation. He records that St. Ambrose himself expressed his high regard "for her truly pious way of life, her zeal in good works, and her regular churchgoing. Often, when he saw me, he would break out in praise of her, congratulating me on having such a mother."

As we can see, in setting out to study the life of a woman saint, we have actually studied the life of two great souls, whose lives and fates were so inextricably intertwined. Indeed, we can say that St. Monica's greatest miracle, was St. Augustine himself! Monica herself did not plead for a miracle; she prayed and sacrificed for the conversion of her son. Her prayers, disappointments, and tears were all means of drawing her closer to God. In her heroic efforts for her son's conversion, she herself became a saint.

Her feast is celebrated on August 27, the day before that of her son, Augustine. The California city of Santa Monica was first visited by missionaries on the Saint's feast day, and was therefore named after her.

Books On St. Monica

- St. Augustine, Confessions
- St. Monica: The Power of a Mother's Love by Giovanni Falbo
- Saint Monica: C. 332-387 : Model of Christian Mothers by F. A. Forbes
- Life of Saint Monica by Em Bougard and Mrs Edward Hazeland
- The life of St. Monica: The mother of St. Augustine by Mary Elizabeth
- History of St. Monica by M. L. Abbe Bougaud
- Forbes Saints' Lives 7 Book Set (Saint Monica, St. Catherine of Siena, St. Athanasius, St. Vincent De Paul, St. Ignatius of Loyola, St. Teresa of Avila and St. John Bosco.)

The **Unknown Baba** lived a hidden life in the Hidden One. Shunning the glare of popularity and the adulation of madding crowds, he lived his simple life in the sequestered vales of anonymity. But many were the lives that were touched by his profound wisdom and grace. He gave the love of his heart to everyone who met him; and he was always ready to share what he had with others. He saw in everyone, the image of the Eternal.

The Unknown Baba

I often think, again and again, of a saint of God. He was a quiet man – he lived a hidden life in the Hidden One; he lived away from the glamour, the noise, the shouts and shows of this world; he was pure and humble and true. He attended to the ordinary tasks of life as an ordinary man: and those who met him did not suspect that they stood in the presence of a holy man. But the Angels above knew it. And, one night, as he was rapt in the ecstasy of communion, the Angels visited him and took the dust of his feet. And as they were about to depart, they said to him: "O saint of God! Let us know what you desire. We would love to leave with you some gift or the other, to mark our reverence for you!"

The saint smiled and said: "I have no desire at all. I have but one longing – the longing to love the Lord to distraction!"

And the Angels said to him: "Do ask for something, if only to make us happy. May we leave with you the wealth of the world ? You seem to be so poor!"

"Wealth is worry!" answered the saint. "What shall I do with it?"

And the Angels said: "May we give you power over men ?"

"Power is poison. I have no need of it!"

"May we give you the gift of reading the minds of men, of knowing their innermost thoughts and secrets?"

"I read the Book of the Heart," the saint answered. "That is enough for me. It contains the whole science of loving!"

"May we give you the gift of prophecy, of knowing what the future hides?" the Angels suggested.

"There is no future for me," was the simple answer of the saint; "and there is no past. I live in the eternal now and here! Free am I from the memories of yesterday and the hopes of the morrow!"

"May we give you the gift of healing?" The Angels asked.

"The Name of my Master is a healer," the saint answered.

One after another, the proposals of the Angels were turned down. Then the Angels conferred among themselves and decided to so bless the shadow of the saint that whenever it was behind him, it would radiate health and happiness and peace to all upon whom it fell: but if the shadow fell in front of him, so that he could see it, no such thing would happen.

And the saint passed through life not knowing himself how much healing there was in his shadow!

I lay a wreath of reverent homage at his holy feet every year, on July 24, in sacred memory of this saint. He shunned the limelight of the world. He rejoiced in belonging to the rank of the "defeated ones". He went deeper and deeper within himself. He became a hidden root. God blessed the root and out of it sprang red, red roses of strange beauty and wondrous fragrance.

I saw him first when I was barely out of my teens. I had just passed through a serious illness and was convalescing. I was anxious to go out for a change of climate but felt too delicate to ask of anyone the favour of their hospitality. He learnt of it and wrote me a kind and loving letter. "My son," the letter read, "if you would care to come to me, I shall gladly share my room and my meals with you. And I shall serve you and be blessed."

I felt astonished to receive such a letter from one whom I had never seen and who had never seen me. And yet it was not the letter of one stranger to another. Something within me whispered that he was a long-lost friend, an elder brother of times gone by, beyond living memory. I could not resist the simple invitation. I made ready to leave. And when the train steamed into the platform, I looked for him whom I had not seen before. There he was: I knew it was he! For as I looked at him long and deep, a flame kindled within me and I recognised him! And though this incident occurred very many years ago, it still seems as though it happened just yesterday.

He greeted me as a father would greet his son. And spontaneously, I addressed him as "Baba..." The word means "father". Later on, I learnt that he was actually called "Baba" in the small circle of devotees who visited him every evening. Not many knew him: very few understood him: some, indeed, called him "mad". But he did not care. He moved on the pathways of life, blessing all, giving the service of love to all who were in need. He thought little of this world: his heart was absolutely devoted to God. Of God he thought: to God he dedicated his daily work: and not unoften, I found him communing with God, within the veil of silence, and conversing with Him as a friend would speak to his friend, as a servant would speak to his master.

One day, as I sat before him with a look of distraction on my face, he asked: "What are you thinking of, my son?"

And I said: "Baba! I do not even know what I am thinking of. I do not know what I need in this wide, wonderful world."

He gazed into my eyes, he looked deep into my heart, then said: "May I tell you, my son, what it is that you need? Your need, your greatest need, your one and only need is – God!"

"How may I reach Him?" I asked. "How may I draw near to God?"

And he said: "If you would draw near to God, turn away from all that stands between you and Him!"

"Tell me more," I said to him, "that I may understand the meaning of your words."

And he said: "God and God alone -- let that be the watchword of your life! You can't have two things — God and the world. Either you seek God or run after the world. The world will, of course, give you many things but will rob you of your precious peace of mind, without which life, even in a palace, becomes a burden. Blessed, indeed, is he in whose heart there is room for nothing save God and whose mind revolves round Him as planets round the sun!"

"What may a man do to be worthy of God?" I asked him on another occasion.

"Two things," he answered. "First, he must die to all creatures; and second, he must die to his passions."

"What is the mark of him," I asked, "who has died to creatures and to his passions?"

And he answered: "The man who has died to creatures is free from the least taint of attachment. Such a man expects nothing from anyone. He passes through life, asking for nothing, claiming nothing, giving gratitude to all that comes to him."

"And the mark of him, who has died to his passions, is that he has risen above those *dwandas*, as they are called in the Gita – pairs of opposites. Pleasure and pain, loss and gain, sunshine and rain, success and failure, cold and heat, mud and gold – all, all, all are alike to him. He seeks not the pleasant: he avoids not the unpleasant. He does not know what it is to love life or to hate death. He rejoices in the Will of God and is not concerned about himself. His will has been merged in the Will Divine. He has committed all he is, and all he has, at the Lotus Feet of the Lord. To such a man, the world is but a moment. The past, the present, and the future do not exist for him: he dwells in Eternity..."

If I were asked to give a brief summing up of the life of Baba, I would say in his own words: "He was dead to all creatures: he was dead to his passions." He was singularly free from attachment to men and matter. One of his sons was a wayward boy. He had fallen in evil company. Baba tried to draw him to the right path, but the boy appeared incorrigible. And, one day, the news came to Baba that the boy had been caught red-handed by the police and would be packed off to jail. Baba was unperturbed: his face showed not the slightest mark of sorrow or anxiety.

One of his friends, who had some 'influence' over the police, offered to help. Baba would not hear of it.

"But, Baba, if the boy is sent to jail, the reputation of the family would suffer," the friend suggested.

"Whose family?" Baba calmly asked. "And whose reputation? These are as shadows on the wall, bubbles floating on water! One thing only is real. It is the Will of God. And whatever He Wills is for our good. If God's Will takes the boy to jail, it will surely do him good!"

The boy was sentenced to a brief imprisonment. And Baba's words were prophetic. The jail term did him good. Today, that boy is an honest citizen of India, earning enough to maintain his family, grateful that he was once sent to jail!

To Baba came both the so called "good" men and the so called "bad" men. He did not discriminate between the two. He gave his love to all! One of the men who visited him, from time to time, was afflicted with a loathsome skin disease – a result of profligacy in his earlier years. His own relatives shunned this man: no one would even as much as draw near to him. He came to Baba as if to his own mother. And Baba always greeted him with a mother's love. Baba called him by the significant name, *'Antaryamin'*, "the Indwelling One…" Baba saw in him, as he saw in every one, an image of the Eternal. Baba washed his sores, bathed his foul-smelling body, gave him clean clothes to wear, fed him and, bowing down to him, give him a silver coin, whenever he had one to spare.

To Baba came many who were in need of material help. He was not a wealthy man, but he was always ready to share with them what little he had: he kept back nothing for himself. Again and again, he emptied himself: God came and filled him. He ate but once in twenty-four hours.

"You eat but once a day," I said to him on one occasion; "and if you do not eat your fill, you must feel hungry all the time!"

What was his answer? "What I share with others," he said, "comes back to me tenfold, and I feel full!"

He kept awake for the greater part of the night, at times, reading aloud from the *Sant-bani* (the words of the saints); at other times communing, in silence, with the Beloved. I tried to keep a vigil with him, but sleep overpowered me and carried me away.

He was ever awake in the deeper sense of the word. "Wake up, O ye who are lost in the slumber of the senses!" he said, again and again. "The night hath come to an end. Do you not realise that with each passing moment someone is passing out of the body and starting upon the inevitable journey? Whose turn will come next, who knows? Wake up! Beware of the temptations of this transient life, and direct your mind and heart to God!"

"It is so difficult to keep awake," I said to him.

The colour of his countenance suddenly changed and his voice was charged with the fury of a storm as he said: "If you cannot keep awake, why don't you put on black clothes as a mark of mourning? Does it befit you to spend your time in feasts and festivals, in foolish merriment and vain rejoicings? It were well for you to hide your face in shame. For I tell you, until you have reached the stage of union with the Beloved you can only weep without ceasing!"

"If you would attain to the Beloved, be asleep even when you seem to be awake!" In our waking hours, we are absorbed in the affairs of the world. Be asleep to the world, Baba said. Be asleep to all that the world stands for. In this sleep the soul is released from the snare of the body. In this sleep memory is lost and attachments and enmities fall off themselves. In this sleep, the poor man forgets his broken cottage and the rich man his luxurious couch. In this sleep there is no fear of the future, no burden of the past, no thought of selfish gain or loss. Live and move in the world as if you are asleep!

"Give me some simple, practical rules," I said to him once, "whereby I may regulate my daily living and enrich my inner life."

And he said: "Three simple rules let me pass on to you. If you will live up to them, your life will bloom as a garden in spring, blessing all who cross your pilgrim-path:

1. Talk a little or not at all. And when you open your lips, see that your talk concerns God.
2. Judge no one! Behold the good in all! Every one whom you see or meet has something good to teach you. Learn of him in all humility. Criticise no one. Give your love to all and give the service of love to all. And, even in your secret thoughts, send your goodwill and good wishes to all.
3. Do not depart from the truth. Though you are cut into pieces, do not flinch in your loyalty to the truth."

It was my great good fortune to have stayed with Baba for a fortnight. He served me as only a mother can serve her child. He blessed me as a mother would bless her only child. He gave me the love of his holy heart. He taught me how to sit in silence and, entering into the depths within, rise above time and space and be absorbed in the One Name of the Beloved. "Repetition of the Name," he said to me again and again, "is perhaps the simplest and the most effective *sadhana* (spiritual discipline) you can practise." And he asked all who came to him to repeat, again and again, the Name of God, the Holy Name. He himself spent several hours of the day and night in repeating the Name of God and in reading aloud the *Sant-bani* and the *Gurbani*, the inspired utterances of the Saints and the Gurus of Humanity.

When the time came for me to take leave of him, I bowed low and clung to his feet. Tears rolled out of my eyes in an unending stream. And I said to him: "My heart is sad, for the time has come when I must leave you. For fifteen days, your shadow has been a shining light upon my face. And now I must go…"

The memory of this man, whom I refer to in all love and reverence, as 'the Unknown Baba' has been a source of ceaseless blessing to me and a light upon my path!

Martin Luther King Jr.

Martin Luther King Jr. was the inspiration and driving force behind the American Civil Rights Movement. Time magazine nominated him as the American of the year in 1963. In 1964, he became the youngest recipient of the Nobel Peace prize. A visionary leader and a messiah of liberation for his people, he became a martyr to the cause of racial equality and the establishment of civil rights for blacks. Today his name is remembered as the leader of America's greatest non-violent movement for justice, equality and peace.

Martin Luther King Jr.

The life of the great-souled leader which I am about to narrate to you, takes us back to the dark days of racial intolerance and deeply entrenched colour prejudice in the world's most powerful democracy. I am referring to the United States of America in the 1950's – a time when the equality of all men envisioned in the historical *Declaration of Independence* was far from a reality. Blacks, Hispanics, and Asians were discriminated against in many ways – overtly and covertly. The 50's were a turbulent period in the history of America – and the blacks rose to fight for a new Civil Rights Movement.

Martin Luther King Jr. was the driving force behind the movement. On August 28, 1963, he led a huge rally in Washington D.C. and on the steps of the Lincoln Memorial, delivered a famous speech that has gone down in history as the "I have a dream" speech. Let me quote from this unforgettable oration:

This is no time to engage in the luxury of cooling off, or to take the tranquilizing drug of gradualism.

Now is the time to make real, the promise of democracy. Now is the time to rise from the dark, desolate valley of segregation to the sunlit path of racial justice. Now is the time to lift our nation from the quick sands of racial injustice to the solid rock of brotherhood. Now is the time to make justice a reality for all God's children...

I say to you today, my friends, even though we face the difficulties of today and tomorrow, I still have a dream...

I have a dream that one day this nation will rise up and live out the true meaning of its creed: "We hold these truths to be self-evident: That all men are created equal."

I have a dream that my children will one day live in a nation where they will not be judged by the colour of their skin – but by the content of their character...

I have a dream ...

Today, we remember Martin Luther King, who became a martyr to the cause of racial equality and the establishment of civil rights for blacks.

Martin Luther King Jr. was born on January 15, 1929, in Atlanta, Georgia. His grandfather and father had both been pastors of the Ebenezer Baptist Church in Atlanta, and from 1960 until his death, Martin Luther acted as co-pastor of the same church alongside his father.

He was the second child and first son to the Reverend Michael Luther King and Alberta Williams King. He had one sister, Christine and one brother, Alfred Daniel. He was actually named Michael, after his father, at birth. When the family visited Germany in 1934, his father changed both of their names to Martin in honour of the great German Protestant leader, Martin Luther.

When he was six years old, and playing with other children in the neighbourhood, he found the game rudely interrupted by a woman, who dragged away his playmates and said to him, "From today onwards, don't you dare play with my children." To say that young Martin was stunned at this outburst would be to understate the case. He was deeply hurt and burst out crying. He wondered, "We were playing so happily together. I did not trouble my friends in any way. In fact I was very fond of them. They too, reciprocated my feelings. Then, why am I being stopped from playing with them?"

He ran to his mother, laid his head on her lap, and began to cry softly. With a sob he asked her, "Mother, why did that woman ask me not to play with the children of the neighbourhood?"

Said the mother softly, "It is because we are black. They are white-skinned and we are black. My son, remember one thing, your skin maybe black, but that does not matter, because you are no less than anyone else. God, who is present within them, also resides within you. Do not worry. If that lady does not want you to play with her children, then you must not play with them."

My friends, this incident had a deep impact on the child. So many questions arose in his mind. These thoughts plagued him again and again, "Just because I am dark-skinned, I am not allowed to play with white children. Why is that so? What is the difference between them and me? Why can we not play together?"

Black Africans had come to America during the 17th and 18th centuries. Many of them had become slaves, working for rich white plantation owners. As years passed, many of the blacks were subjected to inhuman treatment, and deprived of all rights and basic human dignity.

It is said that when Abraham Lincoln was a young man of about 18, he saw a young negro girl being auctioned. When he learnt of the cruel custom of buying and selling slaves, he was deeply saddened, and vowed that he would do all he could to put an end to this barbaric custom of slavery. God gave him the opportunity he sought, and this humble boy, born in a log cabin, became the president of the United States. With his dedicated efforts, finally slavery was abolished. However, white people continued to treat the blacks shabbily. If a white person was walking on the road, a black man could not walk alongside. In trains, there were carriages wherein blacks could not sit. There were many restaurants only for whites; blacks were forbidden to enter. There were many schools where black children could not get admission.

Like several young black boys and girls of his generation, the young Martin attended segregated public schools in Georgia, where black children were kept apart from the whites. After passing out from school, he went on to receive a B.A. degree in 1948 from Morehouse College, a prestigious Negro institution of Atlanta, from which both his father and grandfather had graduated. He then undertook three years of theological study at Crozer Theological Seminary in Pennsylvania where he was elected president of a predominantly white senior class, and awarded the B.D. (Bachelor of Divinity) in 1951. He won a fellowship at Crozer, which enabled him to enroll for postgraduate studies at Boston University, where he received a doctorate in Systematic Theology. The following year, he accepted the pastorate at Dexter Avenue Baptist Church in Montgomery, Alabama. In Boston, he met and married Coretta Scott, described by his biographers as "a young woman of uncommon intellectual and artistic attainments". The Kings were blessed with two sons and two daughters.

In Montgomery, an incident happened, which changed the young pastor's life completely. One day a black woman named Rosa Parks was travelling by bus. There was an understanding that if the seats in the bus were fully occupied when a white person boarded, then a black passenger had to vacate the seat to make room for the white person. So it happened to Rosa. A white passenger entered the bus, and Rosa was asked to vacate her seat. The black lady retorted, "Why should I move from my seat? I boarded this bus earlier, and I took this seat first. I have paid for and bought my ticket so why should I get up from my seat?" This was something unprecedented in the state of Alabama, where segregation was stringently implemented in all buses. There was a tremendous uproar, and Rosa Parks was forcefully made to get off the bus and taken into custody.

On that very day, December 5, 1955, black residents launched a protest and elected King as president of the newly-formed Montgomery Improvement Association. Martin Luther had read the book on Civil Disobedience written by Thoreau and was deeply influenced by it. In his book, Thoreau had written about the concept of 'Passive Resistance'. Martin was also a great admirer of Mahatma Gandhi, and his doctrine of non-violence and non-cooperation. He now decided that he would adopt the way of passive resistance and encouraged the blacks to boycott all bus services until justice was assured to them. The boycott continued throughout 1956, and King gained national prominence for his role in the campaign. In December 1956, the United States Supreme Court declared Alabama's segregation laws unconstitutional and Montgomery buses were desegregated.

Determined to build upon the success in Montgomery, King and other southern black ministers founded the Southern Christian Leadership Conference

(SCLC) in 1957. In 1959, King toured India and further developed his understanding of Gandhian non-violent strategies. Later that year, King resigned from Dexter and returned to Atlanta to become co-pastor of Ebenezer Baptist Church with his father. He gave full credit to Mahatma Gandhi as the leader who inspired his protests, and vowed that he would continue to adopt Gandhian methods in his fight for racial equality.

In the spring of 1963, King and SCLC lead mass demonstrations in Birmingham, Alabama, where local white police officials were known for their violent opposition to integration. Clashes between unarmed black demonstrators and police armed with dogs and fire hoses generated newspaper headlines throughout the world.

During this struggle, he was put in prison several times. Once when he was in prison, someone dropped a fire bomb in his house. Though the house collapsed, by God's grace, his wife and newborn baby escaped without a scratch. When the blacks came to know of this, they got together in thousands. They were furious with rage. They wanted to confront the whites. If they can stoop to violence, then we will also retaliate with violence, they screamed angrily.

But, like Mahatma Gandhi, Martin Luther requested them to counter hatred with love. The power of violence is far inferior and weaker as compared to the strength of non-violence, he reasoned with them. Let us send out peaceful vibrations. You continue to give love and tolerance to the whites, he taught them.

Once, a few whites filed a false court case against Martin Luther. The judge passed a verdict against him, laying a fine on him. Martin Luther said, "I will not pay the fine. When I have not done any wrong, then the question of paying a fine does not arise." The judge told him, "If you do not pay the fine you will have to go to jail." He said, "I do not mind, you can send me to prison."

When the black people came to know of this, again they gathered together in thousands and surrounded the courthouse. Seeing this, the police officers were frightened. They say, "If we pass through this crowd with Martin, on the way to the prison, these people will not spare us." So, the police officers themselves pooled out the money from their pockets and paid the fine for Martin and freed him.

Martin Luther King always remained firm in his resolve and stuck to his ideals. With his persistent efforts, President Kennedy responded to the Birmingham protests by submitting broad civil rights legislation to Congress, which led to the Passage of the Civil Rights Act of 1964. But before the president could sign it, he was assassinated. That night Martin Luther King cautioned his wife, "In a short while the same is going to happen to me."

The Civil Rights Bill was subsequently signed by President Johnson. But King's work was not yet over. Subsequent mass demonstrations culminated in the *March on Washington for Jobs and Freedom* on August 28, 1963, in which more than 250,000 protesters gathered in Washington, D. C. It was on the steps of the Lincoln Memorial that King delivered his famous "I Have a Dream" speech, which I have quoted earlier. Martin Luther's words touched a chord in the hearts of the people.

Very soon, he grew famous. Time magazine nominated him as the American of the year in 1963. In 1964, he became the youngest recipient of the Nobel Peace prize. However, along with the fame and accolades came conflict within the movement's leadership. Malcolm X's message of militant black nationalism resonated with northern, urban blacks more effectively than King's call for non-violence; King also faced public criticism from "Black Power" proponent, Stokely Carmichael.

King's campaign was not only weakened by divisions among the black leadership, but also by the increasing resistance he encountered from national political leaders. FBI director, J. Edgar Hoover's extensive efforts to undermine King's leadership were intensified during 1967 as urban racial violence escalated, and King's public criticism of U.S. intervention in the Vietnam War led to strained relations with Lyndon Johnson's administration.

In late 1967, King launched a Poor People's Campaign designed to confront economic problems that had not been solved by earlier civil rights reforms. The following year, while supporting striking sanitation workers in Memphis, he delivered his final address, "I've been to the Mountaintop." His extemporaneous speech focused on the necessity to keep up the struggle despite the still-bleak economic and racial conditions. His conclusion first reflected on his near-brush with death in 1958, and then his thunderous assertion followed: "Like anybody, I would like to live a long life—longevity has its place. But I'm not concerned about that now. I just want to do God's will. . . And so I'm happy tonight; I'm not worried about anything; I'm not fearing any man. Mine eyes have seen the glory of the coming of the Lord." The next day, April 4, 1968, King was assassinated.

Today his name is remembered as the leader of America's greatest non-violent movement for justice, equality and peace. Martin Luther King Jr. was one of those rare men in history, about whom it could be said that his integrity and commitment to the cause of service was total and absolute. All his life, he remained true to his philosophy and methods of non-violent conflict-reconciliation and social change. Through the example of his life, he taught us to treat all people with equal respect and love and affection and to go out of our way to help others. His life was multi-hued with the colours of love and empathy.

I pray that our life too may be filled with love for mankind, for bird and animal so that by God and Guru's Grace our life may be useful and purposeful!

Sayings of Martin Luther King Jr.

I refuse to accept the view that mankind is so tragically bound to the starless midnight of racism and war that the bright daybreak of peace and brotherhood can never become a reality.... I believe that unarmed truth and unconditional love will have the final word.

* * * * *

The time is always right to do what is right.

* * * * *

Everybody can be great. Because anybody can serve. You don't have to have a college degree to serve. You don't have to make your subject and your verb agree to serve.... You don't have to know the second theory of thermodynamics in physics to serve. You only need a heart full of grace. A soul generated by love.

* * * * *

I have a dream that my four little children will one day live in a nation where they will not be judged by the colour of their skin, but by the content of their character.

* * * * *

A genuine leader is not a searcher for consensus but a moulder of consensus.

* * * * *

All labour that uplifts humanity has dignity and importance and should be undertaken with painstaking excellence.

* * * * *

I just want to do God's Will. And he's allowed me to go to the mountain. And I've looked over, and I've seen the promised land! I may not get there with you, but I want you to know tonight that we as a people will get to the promised land.

Books By Martin Luther King Jr.

- *The Autobiography of Martin Luther King, Jr.* by Martin Luther King Jr. and Clayborne Carson
- *A Testament of Hope: The Essential Writings and Speeches of Martin Luther King, Jr.* by Martin Luther King and James M. Washington
- *I Have a Dream: Writings and Speeches That Changed the World* by Martin Luther King
- *Strength to Love* by Martin Luther, Jr. King
- *The Measure of a Man (Facets)* by Martin Luther, Jr. King
- *Why We Can't Wait (Signet Classics)* by Jr., Dr. Martin Luther King and Jesse Jackson

Books On Martin Luther King

- *The Story of Martin Luther King Jr.* by Johnny Ray Moore and Amy Wummer
- *Happy Birthday, Martin Luther King Jr. (Scholastic Bookshelf)* by Jean Marzollo and J. Pinkney
- *Martin Luther King, Jr. (Real People)* by Pam Walker
- *Martin Luther King, Jr.: A Life (Penguin Lives Biographies)* by Marshall Frady
- *Who Was Martin Luther King, Jr.?* by Bonnie Bader and Nancy Harrison
- *A Picture Book of Martin Luther King, Jr. (Picture Book Biography)* by David A. Adler and Robert Casilla
- *Martin's Big Words: The Life of Dr. Martin Luther King, Jr.* by Doreen Rappaport and Bryan Collier
- *Martin Luther King, Jr. (DK Biography)* by Amy Pastan
- *Meet Martin Luther King, Jr. (Landmark Books)* by James T. De Kay

Chandana

Chandan Bala saw, felt and experienced the gamut of the fickle wheel of fortune in her young life. Born a princess, this tender young girl was sold into slavery and suffered abuse and exploitation at the hands of cruel women, before Lord Mahavira came to keep His destined appointment with her, opening the gates of liberation for this remarkable saint.

Chandana

When the great *avatara purushas* walked upon this earth, many were the lives that were touched, even transformed utterly, through just a momentary contact with them. Such is the power of a realised soul, that it can offer deliverance and liberation to so many at a glance, or through a chance meeting! In His Infinite mercy, God endowed Vasumati with such transforming power. Born a Princess, sold into slavery, ill-treated by her mistresses, disfigured and deformed because they envied her beauty, Vasumati at long last had the good fortune to have a glimpse of Lord Mahavira. In that instant, Lord Mahavira recognised her innate goodness, and Vasumati became Chandan Bala, a saint venerated by all Jains today.

Vasumati was the daughter of King Dadhivahana, who was the ruler of the historic kingdom of Anga, which had, in the long forgotten past, been ruled by Karna of Mahabharata fame. He and his Queen, Dharini, lived with their beautiful and charming daughter, Vasumati, in the capital city of Champa.

The neighbouring kingdom of Vatsa, was ruled by King Shatanik, who lived in his capital, Kaushambi, along with his chief queen, Mrigavati. Both the queens, Mrigavati and Dharini, were daughters of Maharaj Chetak of Vaishali republic. The two royal families continued to maintain cordial relations, and lived in peace and prosperity. However, trouble was lurking; for Shatanik was jealous and greedy for greater power. He nourished secret ambitions of annexing his neighbouring kingdom by aggression and invasion – notwithstanding the fact that it was his own brother-in-law, a wise and virtuous man, who ruled the kingdom.

An opportunity for his evil plans was presented to him very soon. Once, when King Dadhivahana had gone with his army to assist a neighbouring king, Shatanik attacked Champa. The kingdom and its capital were defenceless in the absence of the ruler and his army. The cruel soldiers of Kaushambi plundered Champa. In those days, looting was considered to be the reward for all soldiers, and even higher ranking officers would join the plunder and take away whatever they could lay their hands on.

A leading officer of King Shatanik's army, that is, his General and Chief Charioteer, led the plunder of the royal palace of Champa. His name was Kakmukh. He was more interested in acquiring concubines from the vanquished kingdom, rather than mere riches. When he entered the royal apartments, his eyes fell on Queen Dharini. He kidnapped Queen Dharini and Vasumati and swore that he would take the Queen as his mistress and approached her menacingly. When he attempted to violate her chastity, Queen Dharini committed suicide. Princess Vasumati, who was just a little girl, was utterly distraught. The sight of the little girl and the heart-rending death of the queen, brought about a change of heart for Kakmukh. He consoled the weeping princess and reassured her that she would come to no harm from him, and that he would do everything he could to protect her.

When he returned to Kaushambi, he offered the girl to his wife as a gift from the war. His hope was that she would accept the young girl as a daughter, for they were childless. But his wife was hard hearted, and did not appreciate his gesture. She would have preferred that he had brought gold and silver as the spoils of his victory, like other soldiers. Moreover, she was struck by the girl's great beauty and grace, and grew jealous of her.

"I do not need a servant like her," she said to her husband coldly. "She doesn't look as if she is capable of much work. Moreover, I distrust her looks. I do not want her in my home. Take her away and sell her to someone as a slave. May be she will at least fetch us a decent sum of money."

Kakhmukh was saddened that he could not keep his promise to Vasumati. He had been responsible for kidnapping her from the royal palace. He had also been responsible for her mother's death. He would have loved to make reparation for this heinous act by being a father to the orphaned child; but it was not to be. Vasumati consoled him: "Do not grieve for me, dear sir," she said to him. "All that is happening to me is as a result of my past *karma*. You are not responsible for my fate. Take me and sell me, as your wife says, and I will not hold it against you." He too, could not stand up against his wife's wishes. So he decided to auction Vasumati in the open market.

In those days, trading of slaves was a common practice. People could buy and sell slaves like commodities. The one who bought a slave would become the lord and master of the slave. The master would 'possess' his slave, body and soul. He could get any work done from the slaves, treat them any way he wished and nobody could interfere. Kakhmukh took Princess Vasumati to the market and began to auction her in public. He shouted, "Is there anyone who will buy this beautiful and charming girl? I am ready to sell her for twenty thousand gold *mohurs*."

The highest bidder for the girl was a courtesan, who kept a house of ill-repute in Kaushambi. She took one look at Vasumati, and realised that the girl would be an asset to her. "I will give you thirty thousand *mohurs* for her," she said to Kakhmukh. "I shall train her in singing and dancing and in all feminine charms, that she will soon become the most sought after courtesan in Kaushambi!"

Vasumati trembled on hearing these words. She fell at Kakhmukh's feet and said to him with tears, "Sir, you promised me refuge and protection when I lost my mother! I beg you, do not push me into a fate worse than death! I would rather die at your hands than be sold as a courtesan."

Kakhmukh was moved by her pleas, and rejected the courtesan's offer. Luckily for him, a rich merchant called Dhanvaan happened to come along at that time. He was also struck by Vasumati's beauty, and offered to buy her. "Give her to me without fear," he said to Kakhmukh. "I shall bring her up as my own daughter!"

Vasumati was sold to the merchant. But his honourable intentions could not come true. Yet again, the merchant's wife took an instant dislike to Vasumati. "Treat her like our daughter? You must be out of your mind," she said to her hapless husband. "No one buys daughters from the slave market. You have paid an extravagant price for her, and I shall get my money's worth out of her. She will be my servant and slave."

Helplessly he watched, as the girl was reduced to hard work and misery. She, who had once been a princess and could have got whatever she wished for, with dozens of servants to wait on her, was now reduced to being a servant herself. Vasumati had to sweep the floor, wash the utensils and clothes, bring wood from the forest, and look after the cattle. In return, she was provided stale food to eat and torn clothes to wear. But the gracious and charming princess never uttered a word of complaint. Dhanvaan was heartbroken to see the plight of the girl whom he had brought home as a daughter. But once again, Vasumati consoled him. "Be not grieved, dear father," she said to him. "All that is happening to me is the result of my own past *karma*. I accept it all as the Will of God."

Years passed, and Vasumati grew up to be a beautiful and attractive young maiden. The merchant's wife grew even more harsh in her attitude. She could never understand her husband's kindness and affection for Vasumati. She was only afraid that he would fall in love with the slave girl, and make her his mistress. She waited for an opportunity to harm Vasumati, and wreak her anger and vengeance upon the beautiful slave.

Once, when her husband had to leave the city on business, she had Vasumati in her power. She shaved off the young girl's hair, beat her up, shackled her hands and feet in iron chains and locked her up in the underground dungeon beneath the house. Then she locked the house and left to visit her parents. She hoped that Vasumati would starve to death by the time she returned.

Dhanvaan returned home earlier than he had anticipated. Seeing his house locked, he enquired after his wife from the neighbours. They informed him that his wife had left home a few days earlier.

"But what about Vasumati?" he asked. "Did she leave with my wife?"

One of the neighbours said to him that he had not seen Vasumati leaving the house. "But I have heard a very faint wail coming from the house last night," she added.

Anxious and desperate, Dhanvaan went round the house, listening carefully at various windows and back doors to see if he could find out anything about Vasumati's whereabouts. At one of the windows, he was startled to hear a feeble cry of pain. Acting quickly, he had the doors of the house broken open and entered within. But Vasumati was nowhere to be found. Where could she have gone? Nobody had seen her leave the place. And what of those wails and cries they had heard?

All of a sudden, the pitiful cry was heard yet again. Dhanvaan was perplexed. Where was it coming from?

"Vasumati! My child, where are you?" he cried out.

He heard a very frail voice answer, "Father! I am here."

The cellars and underground dungeons had been abandoned and disused for long. Therefore, it did not occur to him to go downstairs and explore the nether areas of the house. Strangely disturbed by the tortured wails, he looked around helplessly. At last, he realised that they were emanating from below the house. He rushed down the disused steps to the cellar, and was appalled at the sight that met his eyes.

The girl whom he loved in his heart of hearts as his own child, was locked up in an unventilated dungeon. She was virtually gasping for breath, for the foul underground air was suffocating her. And she was unrecognisable! Her long and lovely hair had been chopped off, and her head had been shaved bald. She had been beaten up and her face and limbs were bleeding. Her clothes were torn and tattered. Her limbs were fettered with strong iron chains!

Horrified and distraught, Dhanvaan cried out, "Dear child! What has happened to you? How were you brought to such a condition?"

Vasumati was in no condition to reply. Only a groan of pain emanated from her lips.

Dhanvaan realised the dire condition she was in. The doors to the dungeon were locked. His cruel wife had taken the keys away, for her intention was to leave Vasumati to perish.

"Do not fear, my child," he reassured her, gathering his wits. "I shall go out and get help. I shall bring the neighbours and a blacksmith who will free you from this dungeon and those cruel fetters. Keep up your spirits, for I shall return to you very soon! You must know that I love you like a father!"

He rushed upstairs to see if there was anything he could offer to the tortured girl. There was nothing in the house – not a drop of water, not a grain of food! He found a few green grams (*channa*) in the kitchen, and he took it down to her in a basket. "Dear child, eat a few of these," he begged her. "Keep up your spirits! I shall free you soon from your misery!"

And he rushed out of the house to get help.

But God had other plans for Vasumati! In order to tell you about these plans, I am now constrained to leave Vasumati fettered and shackled and confined in the dungeon, and go back in time...

Lord Mahavira had arrived in Kaushambi sometime earlier. He had been welcomed by the people of the city, and was offered hospitality for his followers and *bhiksha* for himself by all the leading citizens. But he had graciously declined all the invitations and announced that he would go on a fast. He was in the 12th year of his spiritual life at that time, and the vow he took was unprecedented: "I will break my fast only when I accept alms from a starving, shaven-headed princess-turned-slave in fetters, dressed in tattered clothes, who offers me green grams with both smiles and tears," he announced, to the consternation of his devotees and all the assembled people. Would his fast ever be broken under such impossible conditions?

Five months and twenty six days after he began fasting, Lord Mahavira opened his eyes and heard Vasumati's cry in his heart. He got up from his meditation and proceeded straight to the house of Dhanvaan, without anyone to show him the way. He encountered Vasumati at her prison. At that moment, a miracle came to pass. The doors to the dungeon opened of their own accord and her fetters broke away. Week and emaciated as she was, the moment she met his eyes, such joy flooded Vasumati that she forgot all her sorrows and tried to stand, smiling at him in welcome. But Lord Mahavira seemed to turn away! The poor girl began to cry. At this, he turned back, for all his conditions were now met. Here was a princess-turned-slave in fetters, with a shaven head and in tattered clothes, smiling and crying all at once! In her hands, she held a basket of green grams which was all she could offer to him at that moment in time! Her fetters fell off and the Mahashraman broke his fast at last!

In the meanwhile, Dhanvaan returned with the neighbours. He was indeed wonderstruck by Vasumati's wisdom and forbearance. She had shown mercy even towards those who had behaved badly with her. Dhanvaan embraced Vasumati and said to her, "My dear Vasumati! You are like a piece of sandalwood. One may cut or crush or rub sandalwood; but it only spreads fragrance all around in return. Hence, I shall call you Chandana from today."

When Sri Mahavira obtained enlightenment, many people came to him and became his disciples. But Vasumati was his first disciple, who devoted herself at the lotus feet of the master and served him faithfully.

There is a lot that this young girl's life can teach us. We are easily annoyed and upset by every little inconvenience that we have to face. We become angry and frustrated by the ordinary problems of life and start complaining bitterly. We get disturbed and we upset others as well. We must also learn to say, like Chandana, "Whatever is happening to me is a result of all my *karmas*. Why should I blame anybody else?" If only we could understand this well, that whatever occurs in our lives, is a result of our previous *karma*, then it will be easier to live our lives in peace and bring peace and happiness to those around us.

Books On Chandana

- *Jainism and the New Spirituality* by Vastupal Parikh
- *Princess Chandanbala* by Saritá Sádhví

Milarepa

Milarepa is venerated as a Tibetan *yogi*, who gave new meaning to the concept of *Guru seva* and *Guru bhakti*. After an early life of stormy and dark passions, he sought the Supreme Truth at the feet of his Guru. Against all odds, he finally won the Guru's grace and was accepted into the discipleship which eventually paved the way for his Liberation.

Milarepa

*M*ilarepa, the great yogi of whom I am about to tell you, is held in veneration by Buddhists and Hindus alike. He symbolises the very essence of *guru seva* and *guru bhakti* – that is, service and devotion to the Guru.

The Guru is often required to be a hard task master for the sake of his disciple. He who expects a 'soft' treatment from his Guru, can never hope to tread the hard and thorny path to Realisation. But we must remember that a Guru who seems harsh and cruel is actually being kind and gracious to us! For it is not an easy task to prepare a disciple – even the best among them – for liberation. The veil of ignorance with which we cover ourselves must be torn asunder. The ego which is the greatest obstacle at the entrance to the spiritual path, must be shattered and utterly destroyed. The heavy weight of bad *karma* that we carry with us from our many previous births, and to which we keep on adding in our current life, must be neutralised. And this is only one half of the story! When the 'black' board of our life has been wiped clean of its accumulated dirt and filth, it must be adorned with all that is beautiful, valuable and worthwhile in us. In place of our former arrogance and presumption, the Guru must bring out our innate humility and self-effacement. The vices and evil habits of a lifetime must be obliterated, and mild and gentle virtues brought in their place. Haste, rashness and the impulse to take short-cuts must be replaced by tolerance, patience and the spirit of acceptance.

It is not an easy task to prepare the disciple for the spiritual journey! Most true disciples will tell you how they passed through their own ordeal of fire — their personal *agni pariksha* — before they were accepted, initiated by the Guru.

What an ordeal Milarepa had to pass through before he attained the grace of the Guru! His determination and perseverance are truly heroic, and serve as an inspiration to millions of seekers even today — a whole millennium after his life.

Milarepa is thought to have been born around the year 1052 A.D. in the Gungthang province of Tibet. His father, who was a wool trader, became wealthy and prosperous when his son was young. He built a three storey mansion in the small mountain hamlet where they lived. He was a kind, generous and hospitable man, and the entire village was invited to attend the feasts and banquets which were often held in his house. His brother and sister, who also lived in the vicinity, benefited from his munificence. He shared all he had with them liberally; and the more he gave away, the more he seemed to prosper. Milarepa and his sister Peta thus grew up in an environment of plenty and prosperity. They lacked nothing, they wanted nothing.

When Milarepa was still very young, his father suddenly fell ill. Calling his brother and sister whom he had supported all their lives, he made a final request: that they should care for his family even as he had cared for them in his lifetime; that his house, his estate and all his possessions should be managed by them until Milarepa came of age, and could take possession of his inheritance. He died soon thereafter, and his property was put under the guardianship of his brother and sister.

The greed of wealth can lure good people astray; Milarepa's uncle and aunt were greedy, unscrupulous and weak-willed. They speedily divided the property among themselves, leaving their brother's family dispossessed, and reduced to utter poverty. The widow and her two hapless children were forced to go to live in a lowly shack and toil in others' fields to earn a pittance. The widow's appeal to her friends and relatives to restore their property to her son fell on deaf ears. The villagers who had enjoyed their father's hospitality, now mocked and jeered at them. The children who had lived in the lap of luxury became pathetic urchins, their clothes dirty and tattered, their heads crawling with lice.

Their mother was heartbroken at the misfortune that had befallen them. Her grief and misery hardened her heart to such an extent, that she became crazy to seek revenge on the relatives who had cheated her children of their inheritance.

When Milarepa was fifteen years old, she said to him, "You owe it to your father and me, to wreak vengeance on those wicked people who have reduced us to such utter penury. I now command you to go to a sorcerer and acquire the art of magic from him through your diligence and effort. My heart and soul will not be at peace until you return and teach a lesson to those who cheated and betrayed us."

And so Milarepa was sent off to a lama, who was thought to be a Master of Magic. Now, such black arts were not really taught to young boys in those days. The young disciples would master a few simple spells and showy tricks and sent on their way. But the lama found Milarepa a devoted and earnest disciple, and when he asked the boy what he wanted to accomplish with black magic, the young lad opened his heart out to him.

The lama was touched by the young boy's story. He sent out some of his older pupils to Milarepa's village to find out if the story was true. When they returned to confirm it, he decided that he would indeed confer the power of sorcery on the young lad, by invoking the deities.

Milarepa was an apt and earnest pupil, and learnt all that was taught to him, performing all the prescribed rites and rituals meticulously.

His wicked uncle and aunt who now occupied the great stone house that once belonged to his father, were celebrating the wedding of their children. All the relatives and neighbours who had conspired to cheat and betray his family, had gathered together at the house, and were indulging themselves in food and drink and merriment. Milarepa cast a spell, and the great stone house came crashing down, killing everyone inside.

When some of the villagers tried to retaliate, his mother commanded Milarepa to send a hailstorm that would destroy all their crops. This too, came to pass, just as she had wished.

But now, Milarepa was deeply repentant at all the death and destruction which he had caused. He felt that he had taken on a heavy debt of bad karma, which he would never be able to repay in a million lives!

Filled with grief and shame, Milarepa returned to the lama – the only Master he knew. He longed to ask him for religious instruction, but did not dare to displease him. He just stayed on, serving the lama faithfully, hoping against hope that he could one day broach the subject of his salvation to the Master.

Shortly after this, the lama was asked to attend to one of his foremost disciples who died after a very brief illness. The lama was deeply grieved. "I have spent my life teaching my disciples the black arts of death and destruction," he lamented. "Surely, I must take *karmic* responsibility for all the evils that have been caused by my pupils!"

Overcome by remorse, he urged Milarepa to seek out a new Guru who would teach him *Dharma* and show him the way to salvation. Milarepa fell at his feet and begged his permission to take to the life of a monk. The Master not only granted him his wish, but also gave him a letter of introduction to a well known lama. He gave the youth gifts to carry to his new Master, and blessed him before sending him on his way.

The second guru received Milarepa gladly and began teaching him Meditation exercises. But suddenly, the guru had an insight that he was not the right teacher for the young man. So he told Milarepa of a great lama whom he knew, and urged the earnest seeker to go to him for further teaching.

This learned Master was none other than the well known lama known everywhere as "Marpa the translator". He was so called because he had been to India to procure the sacred teachings of Buddhism, which he had brought back to Tibet in large bundles of scrolls. He had spent a lifetime translating them into the Tibetan language. Marpa himself had been the chosen disciple of Naropa, widely venerated as a saint in those days.

When Milarepa first heard the name *Marpa* uttered, he felt an electric current course through his veins. It seemed to be a moment of revelation. He felt thrilled; he felt he had taken the first step towards the Liberation that he had so earnestly sought all these years.

Marpa was an enlightened Master. He was blessed with the power of looking into the future. At the time that Milarepa heard his name, Marpa saw in a vision, that his guru Naropa offered him a *dorje* (scepter) made of *lapis lazuli,* a very precious gem. The Guru urged Marpa to clean the tarnished scepter with holy water until it shone in splendour. "When it is polished, when its brilliant radiance is revealed in all its splendour, I want you to raise it up in a banner of victory, so that it may shine on all the sentient beings of the six worlds!" Naropa urged him.

Marpa understood at once, that he was about to have a momentous meeting with someone who would be his chief disciple and successor. He also understood that the process of the young man's initiation would be difficult and tortuous – as the tarnished scepter has indicated.

Milarepa crossed the snow clad mountains of Tibet to make the perilous journey to the remote village of Drowo Lung, where Marpa's monastery was situated. At long last, Milarepa was at his door step, eagerly begging the Master to take him as a disciple. Outwardly Marpa appeared indifferent and disinterested, even rude and rough. "Tell me about yourself," he said curtly, "but pray do not waste my time."

Milarepa swallowed hard. He made up his mind that he would have to confess his past deeds to his guru. As quickly and briefly as he could, he narrated the sad events of his life – the treachery and betrayal of his aunt and uncle, the loss of his inheritance, his mother's maniacal insistence on revenge, and the devastation he himself had brought about with his spells of sorcery.

"Ever since that fateful day, I have lived in utter agony and shame," he said, shedding bitter tears. "Now, I want to atone for those terrible deeds and seek the path of liberation. Will you be so kind as to accept me as your disciple?"

Marpa was staring at the blue beyond, as if he had hardly heard anything Milarepa had spoken. At long last, he said, "It is obvious that your past life makes you unfit for spiritual training . . ."

Milarepa almost sobbed aloud when he heard those words. As impassively as ever, Marpa continued, "I do not wish to appear hard-hearted, so I will give you two options. The first is that you will be offered food and shelter here, in my cottage, until you find yourself a teacher who will accept you. The second option is that I myself will accept you as my disciple – but you must provide for your food and clothing yourself."

"I beg you to accept me as your disciple," cried Milarepa, overjoyed.

"My teaching is very different from learning black magic tricks," Marpa said sarcastically. "Don't jump so hastily into accepting me as your guru. I demand utter and complete obedience from my disciples. If you so much as try to resist my will, I shall cut you to pieces."

"I shall obey you implicitly, unconditionally," Milarepa swore. "I shall never ever resist your will."

"Let us begin right away," said Marpa curtly. He led his new disciple out into the cold mountainside. Near the monastery was an open field, covered in huge scattered rocks and slabs of granite. Beside the field stood a lofty peak, capped in ice and snow.

"I have learnt the secret of True knowledge from my Master, Naropa," said Marpa. "I can promise you enlightenment and liberation in this birth – all I want you to do is complete the one task that I shall assign to you."

"I will! I will!" said Milarepa excitedly. "Command, I shall obey you."

"Can you see the rocks lying around here on the field? I want you to take them and build for me a circular tower on the eastern side of that peak. I hope to use it for my meditations. Tell me when the tower is half complete, so that I can look at it and give you further instructions."

Swiftly, Marpa turned his back and started walking away to the monastery. Milarepa was stunned. The rocks were enormous, and the eastern slope of the peak was steep and slippery. Would he ever be able to accomplish the task?

"I will come to you when the tower is half completed," he called out to the retreating form of Marpa. And then, with determination, he began to lift the rocks, one by one, carrying each one painfully and laboriously up the steep eastern slope.

That evening, as the setting sun cast its purple-orange glow over the snow clad mountains, Milarepa sank exhausted on the rock he had brought up to the peak. His hands were bleeding; his feet were sore; and his back was breaking!

Down below, he saw the monastery, where the monks were gathering for the evening prayer. As the sweet chimes of the bells fell on his ears, he dreamt of the day when he would also be part of the sacred congregation, in the ochre robes of a monk. The dream gave him renewed energy and strength. He ran down the steep slope, determined to work until dark.

When night fell, he went into the village to beg for food, eating whatever people gave him. He then fell into an exhausted slumber, waking up at the crack of dawn to return to his ordained task.

Day after day, he toiled, until the tower was half complete. Then he invited Marpa to take a look at it.

"Hmm," said the Master, surveying the incomplete structure. "I don't think the eastern ridge was the right choice," he said. "Please pull the tower down and take the rocks back to the field."

Milarepa was nonplussed. "Perhaps I did not hear him right the first time," he thought to himself. In any case, he had sworn complete obedience, and he was determined to keep his vow. Now began the back-breaking task of carrying the rocks back to the field.

When the rocks had all been brought down, Marpa said to him, "I would like you to build a semi-circular tower on the western side. Come to me when it is half complete."

The spring thawed into summer; the summer mellowed into autumn; and the harsh winter came to the Himalayan slopes. Milarepa worked ceaselessly until the tower on the western ridge took shape. He then went to call his Master.

"I don't know what possessed me to ask for a semi-circular structure," Marpa exclaimed, when he had reached the top of the peak. "Please tear it down at once."

"Tear it down again?" gasped Milarepa.

"Yes, please, tear it down and get the rocks back on the field and then come to me for further instructions."

Could a guru be so harsh, so cruel and so thoughtless? Milarepa felt that he had chosen a mad man for his Guru. But he quickly reminded himself, that the way of saints was inscrutable. Who was he to question the master's wisdom? His duty was to do or die. Perish he would, but he would carry out the orders of his Guru.

Two years after Milarepa had first set eyes on his Guru, he received the next set of instructions. He was asked to build a triangular tower on the northern side of the peak.

"Gladly will I do your bidding Master," he said to Marpa humbly. "But before I begin work on the tower a third time, let me ask you: is this really what you want?"

Marpa flew into a rage. "How dare you question me thus?" he flared. "Do you know the terrible physical tortures that my Master Naropa had to endure, before he even got to *meet* his guru? And you, with your dark and sinful past, will not carry a few stones up a mountain?"

"I shall return to you when the tower is half complete," pleaded Milarepa.

"You can do exactly as you please," barked the irate Master.

Milarepa was broken and bruised, in mind, body and spirit. With grim determination, he worked through the icy winter. When Marpa was summoned to see the progress of his work, he asked Milarepa angrily, "Why on earth is this structure triangular in shape?"

"But . . . but . . . sire, that is what you ordered yourself!"

"Me? Never! Your black magic tricks are coming back to you, are they? Destroy this tower immediately, for I can feel the presence of evil spirits in it!"

Milarepa felt he was defeated, nay, destroyed. What could he do? Year after year he had toiled, in vain and fruitless hard labour. Where was the peace and grace he had sought at the feet of his guru? And where, oh where was liberation?

The third tower was also dismantled. The rocks had been carried down to the field. Now, Marpa came to tell him, "I have changed my mind. Build me a square tower, nine stories high, right here on this field. I feel I am too old and weak to climb the peak now. And when this tower is complete, you will receive the secret teaching that will ensure your liberation."

"Your wish is my command," said Milarepa heroically, suppressing his outrage. "But I beg of you, that the *guru-patni*, your wife, may be present here as a witness to your instructions."

"Certainly," beamed Marpa. His wife, Dakmema, was summoned, and heard his instructions.

By now, the lama's disciples began to take great pity on Milarepa. When he was trying to move a huge rock to be put in place as a cornerstone to the new tower, they helped him to shift it. Milarepa thanked them, and carried on his work.

When two stories of the tower had been completed, Marpa came to look at it. He stared suspiciously at the cornerstone and demanded, "Pray, what trick of black magic did you use to move that stone? I am sure you didn't do it yourself!"

When Milarepa told him that a few of his fellow disciples had helped him, Marpa flew into a rage. "So, you are prepared to cheat me and deceive me to gain your ends? Take that stone away and put it back in place yourself."

"Take it away? Why, the tower would collapse!"

"Do as you are told — or leave my monastery at once."

Milarepa was dispirited and forlorn, as he began to pull down the tower — yet again.

One day, when the tower was nearing completion, Dakmema came to him. "Do not despair," she said to him kindly. "Your guru knows what is good for you, and will never ever forsake you."

She offered him some balm to apply on his bruised back and limbs. She shed tears to see him broken and bleeding.

"How can you treat the young man so harshly?" she asked her husband later that day. "In all these years, I have never seen you treat any of your disciples so cruelly. I beg you to show him mercy."

"Alright, alright," said the lama affably. "It is enough for me if he builds a shrine of nine pillars on the ground floor of the tower. I will accept it as his offering to me, and give him initiation."

But Milarepa could do no more. He decided that he would run away from the monastery and seek out another teacher. But he had to bid Dakmema a farewell, for she had been like a mother to him.

"Dear son, do not give up now," she pleaded. "You are so close to achieving your goal!"

"It's no use, Mother," wept Milarepa. "I don't think he will ever initiate me. I must find another teacher."

"Let me help you," said Dakmema impulsively. "I often write the Master's letters. I can imitate his handwriting very well. I will write a letter in his name to one of his disciples, asking him to give you initiation."

Early next morning, Milarepa left the village of Drowo Lung to go to the monastery of lama Ngokpa. When the letter was presented, the lama welcomed him warmly and initiated him immediately.

Relieved and happy, Milarepa retired to a remote cave and began to meditate. But, to his utter disappointment, he was filled with disquiet and unease. The peace he sought so desperately, simply eluded him. He knew at once, that salvation could not be his, unless he sought Marpa's forgiveness for deceiving him.

After several days of such mental agony, Naropa came to his cave to seek him out, with an urgent message; the tower and the shrine had now been completed by Marpa himself! And the Master had sent an invitation to Naropa and his new disciple for the consecration of the shrine. They had to leave immediately.

With what mixed emotions, with what alternating waves of hope and despair did Milarepa return to the familiar monastery at Drowo Lung! He felt that all the suffering, all the pain and physical hardship he had undergone earlier, were nothing compared to the anguish and shame he now felt, for walking out on his Master. The remnants of the towers he had built seemed to mock him. His hope for salvation was now in ruins, like those towers!

When he entered the great hall of the monastery, his eyes filled with tears at the sight of Marpa. He fell at the feet of his master, crying, "You were right, sire! My past sins are far too great to allow me to pursue any spiritual discipline. All I seek now is your forgiveness."

Marpa smiled. "Many years ago, just before you first came to me, I saw a vision. It showed me that one who was to be my greatest disciple, would come to me for initiation. But I saw too, that his soul was tarnished with bad *karma*, and it would require drastic discipline and very difficult training to cleanse and purify him. I knew it would be a tough task – but I also realized that it would be the quickest route to enlightenment for him . . ."

"Dear Milarepa," he continued, "you had to go through several ordeals to cleanse yourself of your past *karma*. Therefore, I ordered you to build and then demolish tower after tower. You probably thought I was heartless and cruel. But, my son, I suffered and struggled with you, as you went through your excruciating ordeal. And when your spirits failed, I took on your *karmic* burden and finished the task for you."

"Master, I am overwhelmed by your boundless and unselfish love," cried Milarepa. "I now know that there is no greater power than the grace of the Guru!"

"Your patience, your undaunted zeal and perseverance have earned you enlightenment and liberation, even in this birth," Marpa said to him "May you be so blessed that you will lead many souls to *Nirvana*, with your spiritual insight and discipline."

Milarepa is venerated to this day as the great yogi of Tibet. It is said that at the moment of his death, he uttered this blessing: anyone who hears or utters, even once, the name of Milarepa, will be so blessed that he will never descend into a lower state of being for seven consecutive births.

May this great yogi bless all of us who contemplate his memorable life!

Sayings of Milarepa

I renounced all affairs of this life;
And, no longer lazy, devoted myself to Dharma.
Thus I have reached the State of Eternal Bliss.
Such is the story of my life.

* * * * *

Faith is the firm foundation of my house,
Diligence forms the high walls,
Meditation makes the huge bricks,
And Wisdom is the great corner-stone.
With these four things I build my castle,
And it will last as long as the Truth eternal!
Your worldly houses are delusions,
Mere prisons for the demons,
And so I would abandon and desert them.

* * * * *

The Buddha cannot be found through searching;
So contemplate your own mind.

* * * * *

Property and wealth are like dew on grass;
Knowing this, gladly should one give them away.

* * * * *

Because I cling not to house and family, I am happy;
I need not this or that, so I am happy.
Because I possess the great wealth of Dharma, I am happy;
Because I worry not about property, I am happy;
Because I have no fear of losing anything, I am happy.

Books By Milarepa

- *Songs of Milarepa (Dover Thrift Editions)* by Milarepa
- *Drinking the Mountain Stream: Songs of Tibet's Beloved Saint, Milarepa* by Jetsun Milarepa, Lama Kunga Rinpoche, and Brian Cutillo
- *Sixty Songs of Milarepa* Translated by Garma C.C. Chang Selected and introduced by Bhikkhu Khantipalo

Books On Milarepa

- *The Life of Milarepa: A New Translation from the Tibetan* by Anonymous and Lobsang P. Lhalungpa
- *The Hundred Thousand Songs Of Milarepa* by Garma C. C. Chang
- *Tibet's Great Yogi Milarepa: A Biography from the Tibetan being the Jetsun-Kabbum or Biographical History of Jetsun-Milarepa, According to the Late Lama Kazi Dawa-Samdup's English Rendering* by Gtsan-Smyon He-Ru-Ka, W. Y. Evans-Wentz, Zla-Ba-Bsam-Grub and Donald S. Lopez Jr.
- *Magic Life of Milarepa* by Eva Van Dam
- *Shaman of Tibet: Milarepa-From Anger to Enlightenment 1040-1143 A.D.* by Wisdom Master Maticintin and Heather Hughes-Calero
- *Tibet's Great Yogi Milarepa* by W.Y. Evans-Wentz
- *Milarepa: Songs on the Spot* by Nicole Riggs

Sage Veda Vyasa

Rishi Veda Vyasa is regarded everywhere in India as a divine Guru, a spiritual luminary, whose stature amongst pious Hindus is virtually equivalent to that of the Gods. Every sacred Hindu scripture invokes his name, with reverence and devotion. A great seer, guru, author, poet and philosopher in the Hindu tradition, he is considered as one of the seven *Chiranjeevis* (immortals) who lived for the welfare of the world, and exemplified the *vedic* ideals of righteousness and perfection.

Sage Veda Vyasa

*L*et me begin the story of this great sage by citing a *sloka* from the opening of the *Vishnu Sahasranaama stotram:*

> *Vyaasam Vasishta naptharam*
> *Sakthe pautram akalmasham*
> *Paraasaratmajam vandhe*
> *Shukaththam Taponidhim* ||

I salute him, the great sage Vyasa, the pure and holy one who is the very embodiment of *taposhakti*, who is the great grandson of Sage Vasishta, the grandson of Sage Shakti, the son of Sage Parasara, and the father of Sage Sukha.

In these few lines which open the *Sahasranaama stotram*, the lineage and the divine power of Sage Veda Vyasa is revealed to us: for we are urged to remember that it is through Vyasa's divine grace that this great prayer of adoration has been revealed to us. Not only this, but the Vedas, the Mahabharata, the Brahmasutras, the Shrimad Bhagavatam, and the other great Puranas, have come down to us thanks to the profound wisdom and the infinite grace of this great sage.

Who was Veda Vyasa? There is actually a belief that the name referred not just to one person, but a whole host of great *rishis* and *munis*, whose combined efforts gave us all the above mentioned texts, which form the very foundation of the Hindu faith. But specific reference is made in our scriptures to Veda Vyasa and his origins. So much so, Kulapati K.M. Munshi, the great intellectual and spiritual luminary who was the founder President of the Bharatiya Vidya Bhavan and its Book University, felt it essential to reconstruct the great sage's life from all the available evidence.

It is said that as the *Dwapara Yuga* was nearing its end, and the dreaded *Kali Yuga* was approaching, the *devas,* saints and sages, led by Lord Brahma, prayed to Maha Vishnu, that He must appear in one of his manifestations to counter the menace of Kali, and save the people from its evil effects. Sage Parasara in particular, performed several austerities to gain this boon of the Lord, that He may be born in his lineage, the lineage of Sage Vasishta. The Lord graciously consented, and came upon this earth as Sage Vyasa.

According to scholars, Vyasa, also known as Krishna Dwaipaayana (which literally means 'he of the dark complexion who was born on an island') was the son of the great sage Parasara and a fisherwoman, Matsyagandha, who lived on a small islet in the River Yamuna. It is said that Vyasa was born to her as the offspring of a sacred union with the great sage. Such was the divine ordination, that Vyasa did not go through the pangs and pains of birth; and his mother, Matsyagandha, remained a pure and virtuous maiden even after she gave birth to her son. At a young age, Sage Parasara took away his son, and so blessed the young woman, that she became the Queen of Shantanu, the King of Hastinapura. It is said that when his mother was reluctant to part with him, the young boy promised her that he would come to her whenever she needed his help.

His father took the young boy to the *ashrama* of Sage Gautama, where he was initiated into the rigorous discipline of *brahmacharya*. He travelled with his father to Badrikashram in the Himalayas, the abode of Maha Vishnu in his *avatar* of Nara and Narayana. Here, Vyasa performed severe *tapasya*, and at long last, was blessed with the realisation of the Supreme Truth. His sojourn in these snow-capped peaks earned him the name of Badharayana – i.e. he whose abode is Badhrikashrama.

In those days, the Vedas were all in one mass, inaccessible and incomprehensible to most scholars and sages. With the blessings of Lord Vishnu, Maharishi Yajnavalkya initiated Vyasa into the study of these great scriptures, and Krishna Dwaipayana became Veda Vyasa – he who was able to split (decipher) the Vedas so that they would be accessible to all illumined souls.

Later, in deference to his father's wishes, Vyasa entered the *grihasta ashrama* (married state) by taking as his wife, the daughter of Sage Jabali, named Pinjala. To her was born his true spiritual heir, Sage Sukha, who would continue the lineage of Vasishta.

We all know that Vyasa not only wrote the greatest of all epics, the Mahabharata, but also played an important role in the story: for he was actually the grandfather of the Kauravas and Pandavas. Both Dhritarashtra and Pandu, adopted as the sons of Vichitravirya by the royal family, were actually fathered by him, so that the Kuru dynasty would not end abruptly without heirs. In fact, it was his mother, later known as Satyavati, who appealed to him to help her create the progeny of her sons; through his union with Ambika and Ambalika were born the royal princes; he also had a third son, Vidura, by a serving maid. The Kauravas were the children of Dhritarashtra. The children of Pandu were called the Pandavas. Thus, without Vyasa, there would have been no Kauravas, no Pandavas and no Kurukshetra War – and, of course, no Mahabharata, either.

Everyone of the Kurus held Veda Vyasa in great esteem; though he urged the scions of the Kuru race to adhere to the path of *dharma*, it was only noble souls like Yudhishtira and Vidura who followed his advice. Through these noble characters, he taught us that the ultimate honour and glory are reserved for those who walk the way of virtue and goodness.

It is said that Lord Vishnu Himself manifested His Divinity through Veda Vyasa, for the purpose of codifying the Vedas. The Vishnu Puranam tells us that Vyasa adopted four great sages as his personal disciples and initiated each one into a particular Veda. Thus, Sage Paila was taught the Rig Veda; the Yajur Veda was taught to sage Vaishampayana; Sage Jaimini was taught to master the Sama Veda; the Atharva Veda was taught to Sage Sumanthu.

This classification of the Vedas was accomplished by Vyasa and later the different branches and sub branches (Sakhas) evolved for each Veda over a period of time. It is said that the gods themselves came to hear the original classification of the Vedas from Sage Vyasa, taking the form of his distinguished disciples: for they were well aware that it was Lord Vishnu who had manifested himself in human form, to accomplish this monumental task for the benefit of his devotees! Thus we have the shloka:

Vyaasaya Vishnurupaaya Vyaasaroopaya Vishnave Namo vai Brahmanidhaye Vasishtaaya namo nama:

I salute Vyasa in the form of Vishnu, and Vishnu in the form of Vyasa; for he was the progeny of sage Vasishta; and the embodiment of the true knowledge of Brahman(The Supreme Spirit).

We know too, that in Chapter Ten of Bhagavad Gita (*Vibhuthi Yoga*), Lord Sri Krishna confirms this, when he says "Of all the sages, I am Vyasa." ("Muneempaayanam Vyasa.")

There is a very interesting story told to us concerning the composition of the Mahabharata. When Sage Veda Vyasa undertook its composition, he realised that it would be a monumental task, well beyond human abilities. At this point, Brahma appeared before him and instructed him to invoke Lord Ganesha to assist him in the task. Lord Ganesha readily agreed to write down all that the rishi dictated. But he insisted on one condition; the dictation had to go on and on, without a break. If ever there was a break, Lord Ganesha would give up and leave.

Veda Vyasa was nonplussed. How could he dictate such a massive and complex work without a break? On the other hand, he knew that without Lord Ganesha's help, he could never ever hope to complete it! He thought for a moment, and then agreed to the condition. But he too, laid a condition before his divine 'stenographer': Ganesha should not write down anything, the full significance of which he had not understood.

The conditions were mutually accepted and the monumental task began. As he had anticipated, Veda Vyasa often needed time to compose those stanzas which embodied complex ideas and situations. At such stages, he would deliberately dictate a difficult stanza – and Lord Ganesha was forced to slow down, or even stop his writing, to try and decipher the meaning of what he had just heard. This gave Vyasa the interval he needed to compose further.

This beautiful story only goes to show that the *Mahabharata* is a work of great complexity and profundity!

Many of us may not be familiar with the story of how Vyasa came to compose that other great Purana – the Srimad Bhagavatam. It is said that once he had completed the Mahabharata, Veda Vysa fell into a mood of pessimism and despair. He had set out to compose the great epic for the good of all mankind; and yet he felt that his task had not been completed. Maharishi Narada now appeared before him and advised him to devote himself to singing the glory of Lord Vishnu. Inspired by this message, Vyasa composed the Bhagavatam, and taught it to his son, Maharishi Shukha. As we know, Shukha recited this sacred scripture to Maharaja Parikshit, to enable him to attain Liberation.

Rishi Veda Vyasa is regarded everywhere in India as a divine Guru, a spiritual luminary, whose stature amongst pious Hindus is virtually equivalent to that of the Gods. Every sacred Hindu scripture invokes his name, with reverence and devotion.

The full-moon day of the month of *Aashad* (July–August) is celebrated all over India as the sacred *Guru Poornima* day. On this auspicious day, we bow down to the great Guru Veda Vyasa, and to the ancient tradition of the *Guru Parampara*. We think of Sri Narayana, who imparted Supreme knowledge to Brahma; we think of the *Sanakadi rishis*, His sons; we think of Lord Dakshinamurti, the ultimate Guru; and the lineage of Sage Vasishta – Parasara – Ved Vyasa – Shukha and the succession of Gurus and disciples who have followed them, keeping the great tradition of the *Guru Parampara* alive to this day.

Sri VedaVyasa is veritably a great seer, guru, author, poet and philosopher in the Hindu tradition. He is considered as one of the seven *Chiranjeevis* (immortals) who lived for the welfare of the world, and exemplified the *vedic* ideals of righteousness and perfection.

He is regarded as the origin and the source all the great Hindu scriptures. He is also renowned as the author of the *Brahma-Sutras* – which are concise but complex and profound aphorisms which express the very essence of the *Vedas*.

We are told that when Vyasa was preparing to leave his physical form and depart from this earth, Maharishi Narada went to him and urged him to write the eighteen *Puranas*. Narada told the sage that his task in life would remain unfulfilled if the *Puranas* were not written. Vyasa accepted his advice and composed the ancient Puranas, also setting up the system of teaching them through *Kathas* – the oral tradition of narratives. Thus, his writings filtered down to every level of society, from the highly learned *pundits* down to the illiterate peasants. This was Veda Vyasa's great contribution to the *Sanatana Dharma* – he took the Vedic religion and its great concepts right into the homes and hearts of the masses.

We owe him a deep debt of gratitude for the same.

It is fascinating to note that *all* the great *Acharyas* of the Hindu faith have written commentaries — or *bhashyas* — on Sage Vyasa's *Brahma-Sutras*. The oldest commentary is by Adi Shankara; this was followed by the *bhashyas* of Ramanuja, Vallabha, Nimbarka and Madhva.

The profound truth enshrined in the *Vedas* has been interpreted in different ways by saints, sages and scholars over the centuries. Based on these interpretations, various systems of thought and schools of philosophy have evolved. Among the most important of these are the systems of the four leading *Acharyas* of Hinduism:

1. The advaita philosophy of Adi Shankara Acharya (non-dualism);
2. The *Visishtadvaita* philosophy of Sri Ramanuja (qualified dualism)
3. The *shuddha dvaita* of Sri Madhwacharya. (pure-dualism);
4. The *Shuddha Advaita* philosophy of Sri Vallabhacharya (pure monism).

The word *Acharya* in Sanskrit means a Holy teacher, a spiritual guide or preceptor. The *Acharyas* became the founders of distinct sects of Hinduism, which still follow their precepts and teachings. However, it must be emphasised that all the great *Acharyas* recognise the fundamental authority of the main Hindu scripture —

the *Vedanta Sutras*, the *Upanishads* and the *Bhagavad Gita*, which were the work of Sage Veda Vyasa.

Thus we owe a deep debt of gratitude to this illustrious sage, who was probably the greatest exponent of the spiritual heritage of ancient India. Through his immortal compositions, the knowledge of the Supreme Reality was handed down to our ancestors. Vyasa's eternal message is embodied in the words: "Victory is, where there is *Dharma*".

Books By Veda Vyasa

- *Vedas*
- *Puranas*
- *Mahabharata*
- *Brahma Sutra*
- *Yoga Bhashya*

Books On Veda Vyasa

- *The Mahabharata Of Krishna Dwaipayana Vyasa* by Kisari Mohan Ganguli
- *The Shiva Purana (Saint Veda Vyasa's)* by Sonal Bharara
- *The Secret Teachings of the Vedas: The Eastern Answers to the Mysteries of Life* by Stephen Knapp
- *Tales from Shrimad Bhagavata of Veda Vyas* by S.C.Nirula
- *The Celestial Key to the Vedas: Discovering the Origins of the World's Oldest Civilization* by B. G. Sidharth
- *Seer of the Fifth Veda* by Bruce M. Sullivan
- *Vedic Paradigm* by His Divine Grace A.C Bhaktivedanta Swami Prabhupada and His Holiness Danavir Goswami

Moses

*M*oses was one of the greatest of the Hebrew prophets, who is also venerated by Christians and Muslims. He was designated by the Lord as the Chosen Leader of the Israelites, to lead them out of slavery in Egypt, to their Promised Land. His life is a remarkable saga of adventure, patriotism, piety and undaunted courage. We remember Moses today, as the one to whom God chose to reveal The Ten Commandments.

Moses

The figure of Moses dominates the first five books of the Biblical Old Testament, which constitute the most sacred scriptures of the Jews, and is venerated as the Torah. Moses is not only the most important prophet in Judaism but also considered as a prophet of Islam, Christianity, the Bahá'í Faith, the Rastafari and many other faiths. He was a great leader, lawgiver, and prophet of the ancient Israelites or Hebrews. He was chosen by God to lead Israelites out of their miserable condition of slavery in Egypt, to Canaan, their own Promised Land of Israel. We may well say that it was he who created the true identity of the Hebrews, paved the way for Israel's nationhood and also delivered to them the Ten Commandments.

Moses was a Hebrew, born into the tribe of Levi. The Levites were one of the twelve tribes of Israel. They were regarded as God's spiritual leaders. He was born in Egypt, as the son of Amram and Yochebed of the tribe of Levi. According to the Bible, the name Moses (*Mosheh* in Hebrew) is derived from the phrase "From the water I drew him" (*meshitihu*) (Exodus. 2:10).

How did it come to pass that this great Hebrew saint was born in faraway Egypt? Why were his people slaves in that country?

The Bible tells us that the Patriarch of the ancient Israelites, called Jacob migrated with his family from Asia to Egypt, due to a severe famine in Canaan. The Bible tells us that they were settled in "the land of Rameses" and that they eventually became property owners there(*Genesis* 47:11, 27). We are also told that Jacob's son, Joseph, became a high ranking official in Egypt after he correctly interpreted the Pharaoh's dreams (Genesis 41:39-45). In fact, so well did he manage the affairs of the state, that when the whole region was struck by a famine, the grain stores of the Pharaoh, under Joseph's management, had surplus grain, which could be sold to other nations. Pharaoh was so pleased with his abilities that he made Joseph viceroy (second in command) over Egypt.

With Joseph's help, the twelve sons of Jacob were all settled in the Egyptian province of Goshen. It is said that when their father Jacob, the Patriarch of Israel, died, Joseph had Jacob meticulously embalmed and, with the Pharaoh's permission, led a huge state funeral back to Canaan, with the twelve sons carrying their father's coffin and many Egyptian officials accompanying them. But after Joseph's death, Israelites lost the respect and status they had enjoyed earlier. Their rising numbers were viewed as a threat to the local Egyptian population. Thus, they were enslaved and used as labourers to build the city of Rameses

(Exodus 1:11). In slavery they dwelt in this foreign land, for over 400 years, until Moses liberated them from this condition, and led them out of the land of Rameses and into the Promised Land. The unforgettable story of their journey is told in the Book of Exodus, which literally means, mass departure or migration.

Let us now return to the life story of the man who led the Exodus, in fact, the man who made it possible. When Moses was born to Amram and Yochebed, conditions were really bad for the Jews of Goshen. Bent on harassing them and persecuting them, the Pharaoh had passed a law ordering all the newborn male children of the Jews to be killed by drowning them in the River Nile. Amram and Yochebed already had two other children, Aaron and Miriam; when Moses was born, they took their newborn son and placed him in a basket of reeds and hid him in the tall grasses of the Nile. His sister Miriam, watched over the baby anxiously, from her hiding place, as the basket floated downstream. She saw a group of women and their servants taking their bath in the river. Among them was a princess, the Pharaoh's daughter, who was without an issue. Hearing the baby cry, the princess rushed to rescue him. She named him "Moses", meaning "drawn from the water". Her desire for a son was now fulfilled, and she took the baby away to the palace with her. Miriam, who had watched her baby brother being rescued, ran back to tell her parents that the baby was safe.

Thus it came to pass that this child of Hebrew slaves, condemned to death by drowning by the Pharaoh, was brought up in the splendour of the Egyptian court as the Pharaoh's daughter's adopted son! The princess made certain that he had the best of everything, including education. With hindsight, we may see that it was indeed God's Will that the Jews' future liberator was raised as an Egyptian prince. For, if Moses had grown up in abject slavery with his fellow Hebrews, he probably would not have developed the pride, vision and courage to defy the Pharaoh and lead a revolt against him.

The Bible tells us of three major incidents in the life of Moses, before the Exodus. As a young man, he once came across an Egyptian overseer flogging a Jewish slave brutally. He was so incensed that he killed the Egyptian then and there. Fearing the wrath of the Pharaoh, he fled to the Midian desert, where he found employment as a shepherd for the priest Jethro. Such was his behaviour and conduct that he was married to Zipporah, his master's daughter. They had two sons, Gershom (meaning a *stranger or alien*); and Eliezer (meaning *the help of God*.)

One day, while he was tending his flock on a lonely hillside, Moses was amazed to see a burning bush, which was not being consumed by the fire. When he approached the bush, he heard the Voice of God speak to him: "I have seen the affliction of my people, and I am determined to save them. I want you to go to the Pharaoh, and arrange to get the Hebrews out of Egypt."

Moses was taken aback. "Lord!" he exclaimed, "Who am I that I should go to the Pharaoh, and should bring forth the children of Israel out of Egypt?"

God said to Moses, "I know that the king of Egypt will not let you go, but by a mighty hand. For I will stretch forth My Hand, and will strike Egypt with all My wonders which I will do in the midst of them: after these he will let you go."

And still, Moses hesitated. "I Beseech Thee, Lord," he said, "I am not eloquent; and I have impediment of speech and slowness of tongue."

Thereupon, God advised him to take his brother Aaron with him; Aaron was a fluent speaker, and bold in spirit, and would play the role of spokesman for Moses. God also gave Moses the power to perform miracles, so that the Hebrews would recognise him as God's messenger and servant.

And thus was the destiny of Moses determined. He took leave of Jethro and returned with his wife and children to the land of his birth, Egypt. Accompanied by his brother, Aaron, Moses went to the Pharaoh and informed him that the God of the Hebrews demanded that he should free the Hebrew people. The Pharaoh refused to listen to him. Therefore, Moses, in accordance with God's instructions, used the miraculous staff that God had given to him, and brought about the nine terrible plagues (diseases that spread rapidly and can cause death) of Egypt. It was God's Will that the Egyptians had to pay the price for their ruler's obstinacy and cruelty.

Thus the Egyptians suffered various disasters such as the following: the water of the Nile turned into blood; the people were attacked by successive infestations of frogs, gnats and flies; their cattle were destroyed by disease; they were afflicted by boils; they were attacked by hail, locusts, and darkness. Each plague was so severe that it brought death and misery to the Egyptians; but the Hebrews were safe and unaffected in Goshen.

The tenth plague was the fiercest of all. Angered by the Pharaoh's refusal to listen to Moses' plea, God sent the Angel of Death to kill all the firstborn sons of the Egyptians — as a proof of His strength and power. Once again, the Hebrews were protected; the Angel of Death would pass over their homes. This last plague was the proverbial last straw that broke the Pharaoh's resistance. He was forced to grant the Hebrews permission to leave immediately. This event is still celebrated by Jews as the Feast of Passover.

Now, Moses found himself the leader of an undisciplined collection of slaves, eager to escape from their life of slavery in Egypt, towards their Promised Land and freedom. It was by no means an easy task! Having let them go, the Pharaoh went back on his word, and sent his army to pursue them. The Jews found themselves facing the Red Sea before them, and the might of the Pharaoh's army behind them. Yet again, God worked His miracle. The waters of the Red Sea parted to allow Moses and his people to pass to the other side. But when the Egyptian army tried to follow them, the waters flooded over them and drowned them.

After many ordeals and troubles, the Hebrews came to Mt. Sinai. Here, God commanded Moses to go up to the mountain-top. Up on these heights, He appeared in the form of a cloud of fire, and gave to Moses, the Ten Commandments: a list of moral imperatives that are sacred to the Jews and Christians, but also universally applicable to all devout and pious souls. God spoke them aloud to Moses, and also handed over to him, two stone tablets on which they were inscribed.

The people heard the voices and saw the flames on the mountain; they heard the sound of the trumpets, and saw the mount smoking; and being terrified and struck with fear, they stood afar, and implored Moses to speak to them.

Moses said to the people, "Fear not; for God is come to prove you, and that the dread of Him might be in you, and you should not sin."

The people answered with one voice, "We will do all the words of the Lord, which He hath spoken."

Taking the book of the covenant, he read it in the hearing of the people: and they said, "All things that the Lord hath spoken, we will do, we will be obedient."

The laws that Moses transmitted to the Jews on that momentous occasion embrace far more than the Ten Commandments. In addition to many ritual regulations, the Jews were also instructed to love God as well as be in awe of Him, to love their neighbours as themselves, and to love the stranger– that is, the non-Jew living among them – as themselves as well.

But the sad part of the Exodus was this: only at the very moment God or Moses were actually doing something for them were the Jews loyal believers. The instant God's or Moses' presence was not manifest, they reverted to amoral, immoral, and sometimes idolatrous behaviour. Like a true parent, Moses raged at the Jews when they sinned, but he never turned against them – even when God did! Once when God declared, wrathfully, that He would blot out the Jews and make for Moses a new nation, he answered, "Then blot me out too." (Exodus 32:32).

The journey to the Promised Land was not easy. For as many as forty years Moses wandered in the wilderness of Sinai, with his unruly people: the Jews were not, at that time, the loyal, disciplined, committed and faithful people that they are today. They constantly complained about the food, the climate, and the slowness of their progress towards the Promised Land. Moses was often driven to rage and desperation over their behaviour. Once, he even heard them complain that slavery in Egypt had been better than this wilderness that they were forced to cross now. Battling against all odds, overcoming many obstacles, Moses led the horde of former slaves, shaping them into a nation, which would become synonymous with determination, courage and patience in the future. Many miracles happened along the way. When food supplies ran out, God sent down what was called *"manna"* (spiritual food) everyday for the nourishment of the Israelites. When the people were in need of water, God told Moses to speak to a rock and water would spring from it. Moses' patience was worn down by now; instead of following God's directions implicitly, he struck the rock with his staff. This was to have a devastating effect on his final days.

The saddest event in Moses' life came to pass when God prohibited him from entering the Promised Land of Israel. If this was due to his disobedience of God's command as mentioned above, it was indeed disproportionate to the offence! As they approached the Promised Land, from the heights of Nebo he surveyed the land promised to his forefathers, which would be given to their children. And then Moses, 120 years old, passed away in the land of Moab and was buried opposite Bet Peor.

Despite this personal tragedy, Moses impressed his monotheistic vision upon the Jews with such force that in the succeeding three millennia, Jews have never confused the messenger with the Author of the message. To quote an admiring biographer, "He selected and set them apart for a divine purpose and consecrated them to the highest ethical and moral laws. Only a man with tremendous will, patience, compassion, humility and great faith could have forged the bickering and scheming fractions who constantly challenged his wisdom and authority into an entity. Under his inspiring leadership, the Jews evolved into a nation and a people who have earned the admiration and respect of the world for their fortitude, patience and perseverance.

Sayings of Moses

What you say, happens.

* * * * *

Who am I, that I should go unto Pharaoh, and that I should bring forth the children of Israel out of Egypt?

* * * * *

Fear not: for God is come to prove you, and that his fear may be before your faces, that ye sin not.

* * * * *

O my LORD, I am not eloquent, neither heretofore, nor since thou hast spoken unto thy servant: but I am slow of speech, and of a slow tongue.

* * * * *

I will now turn aside, and see this great sight, why the bush is not burnt.

* * * * *

I pray thee, if I have found grace in thy sight, show me now thy way, that I may know thee, that I may find grace in thy sight: and consider that this nation is thy people.

* * * * *

The LORD will fight for you; you need only to be still.

* * * * *

Come before the LORD, for he has heard your grumbling.

* * * * *

Do not be afraid. Stand firm and you will see the deliverance the LORD will bring you today.

Books On Moses

- *Bible* – the narratives of Moses are in Exodus, Leviticus, Numbers and Deuteronomy
- *Moses* by Sholem Asch
- *Moses: The Man and his Vision* by David Daiches
- *Moses, Prince of Egypt* by Howard Fast
- *Moses and Monotheism* by Sigmund Freud
- *Moses: The Revelation and the Covenant* by Martin Buber
- *Moses: A Memoir* by Joel Cohen
- *Moses: The Father I Never Knew* by Corey Gjerman
- *Moses: A Life* by Jonathan Kirsch
- *Seven Days to the Sea: An Epic Novel of the Exodus* by Rebecca Kohn
- *Moses as Political Leader* by Aaron Wildavsky
- *Alone Atop the Mountain* by Samuel Sandmel

Jhoolelal

Jhoolelal is held in veneration as the saviour and the *ishta devata* of the Sindhi community. Born at a troubled time in Sindhi history, he came as a messenger of God, to preach the values of tolerance, brotherhood and respect for all religions. His spectacular appearance upon this earth and his miraculous deeds to protect his people from forced conversion, are now become part of Sindhi lore and myth.

Jhoolelal

Jhoolelal – Uderolal!
The very name fills Sindhi hearts with love, hope, faith and optimism.
Jhoolelal! Beda Paar!
Whoso utters the name of Jhoolelal-all his works will be fulfilled.

This is a cry which you will hear reverberating when Sindhis unite as one to celebrate their New year, *Cheti Chand.*

The story of Jhoolelal, the *ishta devata* of the Sindhi community, is intimately associated with the life-giving, life-sustaining River Sindhu.

Perhaps it was this perennial river, with its ever-flowing waters, which first attracted aggressors and invaders from across the Hindu Kush mountains. While the early invaders came to conquer and to trade, the later, aggressors were determined to stay and rule over Sindhis with an iron hand.

During one of the darkest eras in the history of Sind, in the Eleventh Century A.D. the people faced a severe spiritual crisis. A cruel and tyrannical chieftain, Makrabkhan, took over the province of Thatta, after killing the ruler, Shah Sahdat Khan. A fanatic, he crowned himself the ruler of the province, giving himself the name Mirkshah.

Ever since the Arab conquest of 711 A.D. conversion has been forced upon the Sindhis. The early Islamic rulers were eager to force their faith upon the peace-loving population of Sind. They used threats, rewards or promises of official patronage to convert Hindus. If all this failed, they used the sword to bring about forcible conversion. Sadly, many people gave in — either for fear of their lives, or to save their loved ones from persecution.

When Mirkshah took over Thatta, the Hindus had to face the worst kind of persecution. Fawning and flattering Islamic courtiers had incited Mirkshah against the Hindus. To tempt him further, they promised him that he would be granted *jannat* (eternal bliss) if he could use his position and power to spread Islam. Spurred on by such incitement, and also under pressure from fanatical *maulvis,* Mirkshah peremptorily summoned the leaders of all Hindu villages in Thatta and told them: "Convert to Islam, or be prepared for death."

This was not just an empty threat; in those feudal times, it was a *shahi farmaan* — an imperial order. Himself a bigot and fanatic, Mirkshah also had the backing of the powerful clergy and the moneyed classes. He actually believed that such forcible, mass conversion, would open the doors of the heaven- world to him.

Fear and panic gripped the Hindu people of Thatta. Not knowing how to respond to the threat at that moment, they begged Mirkshah to give them some time. It was granted to them, in the hope that they would persuade their followers to convert to Islam, without further pressure from the ruler.

Forty days time was granted to them. But alas, what they could achieve in forty days? Their future seemed bleak and comfortless. How could they give up the faith of their ancestors, the faith they were born into, the true and original faith of the Vedic land of the River Sindhu?

In vain they sought the help of powerful Hindus outside Thatta. But such was the terror in which Mirkshah was held, that no one was prepared to come to their aid.

Sore was the plight of these pious people! Like so many of their countrymen before them, they could have easily agreed to turn their back on their religion, and become the recipients of royal patronage and power. But these were firm believers in the Vedic religion who had kept to their faith against all odds. Now they were faced with a bitter choice – surrender their faith, or lose their lives!

In utter despair and grief, the Hindus of Thatta turned to their God. On the banks of their beloved

Sindhu River they assembled; for was not the Sindhu their Mother and life-giver? Was she not the holiest of holy rivers, with her origins in the sacred peak of Mount Kailash? Had not her banks and valleys been sanctified since millennia by the utterance of the sacred Vedas? On these same sacred banks, the Hindus congregated, praying, fasting, taking sacred dips and offering worship to Darya Shah, (the Lord of the waters), seeking protection and help in their hour of suffering.

They fasted, prayed and offered their worship for forty days and forty nights. Their hope was pinned on Him who was, is, and always will be, the Defender of the defenceless – Him whom we still worship as *Deenabandu, Deenanath*.

A miracle came to pass on the fortieth day. They heard the Divine Voice, an *akashvani*, speak to them and promise them that deliverance was at hand for them. The River God, would be born among them as Uderolal at Nasarpur!

And so it came to pass! To Devaki and Rattanchand of Nasarpur, a child was born. It is said that the child revealed its divine identity to its parents when he opened his mouth – and there, they beheld the mighty Sindhu flowing, with an old man, serene, white-bearded, seated on a *pala* fish – a large sized salmon fish unique to the Sindhu. An *avatara* had appeared in answer to the people's prayers!

It is said that the cradle in which the infant was laid, rocked itself to lull him to sleep. Therefore he was called Jhoolelal – The Lord of the Swing. The astrologer who cast his horoscope, predicted that he would be the Light of the Land – and therefore, his parents called him Uday. Holy men who came to visit the Divine child said that his name would ever remain immortal – and hailed him as Amarlal, the Immortal One.

It is believed that when the *vazir* of the region came to see the child, the child turned into a young man, a black-bearded mature man, and then into a white-bearded venerable old man, before his very eyes! The *vazir* who had come to 'investigate' the miracle, bowed in reverence and awe before the incarnation! To his amazement, he saw the triumphant one leap on to a horse and gallop away, a sword upheld in one hand, a flag held in the other!

The *vazir* returned to Mirkshah and told him that Uderolal was no ordinary child. He and his people were not to be trifled with.

A regiment was sent to arrest Uderolal – but they were simultaneously stopped by a flooded river and the burning towers of their own palace. It was as if the elements had combined to warn them of Him whom they sought to harm.

Appearing before the panic-stricken regiment, Uderolal said to them and their chieftain: "He whom you call Allah, and my people call Ishwar, are but One and the same. All Humanity is one creation – His Divine Family. It was His desire that He made some of them Muslims and some of them Hindus. Unity in diversity is what He has ordained – so let it prevail! Do not persecute your Hindu brothers! Let unity prevail among the Sindhi people, so that Hindus and Muslims can exist in peace and harmony!"

Mirkshah was overwhelmed by the Divine injunction, and promised to follow the command of the *avatara purusha*. The fanatical tyrant has been transformed for life!

The Hindus of Thatta built a temple to honour Uderolal – and the Muslims, for their part, built a Mausoleum close at hand. To this day, both communities worship at these shrines – the Hindus lighting lamps, the Muslims, saying their prayers. It is believed that Uderolal, mounted on his horse, was miraculously swallowed up by the earth opening underfoot at this very spot.

The Hindus hail their saviour as Jhoolelal, Amarlal and Uderolal. The Muslims revere him as Zinda Pir.

The auspicious day of *Cheti Chand* – the full moon day in the month of *Chaitra* – brings with it, dual celebrations for Sindhi Hindus – the New Year day according to the Hindu lunar calendar and the *janam din* (birth anniversary) of their *ishta devata*, the Defender of their faith, Jhoolelal.

From then, to now, Sindhis have passed through many trials and tribulations. They have left behind their homeland; their mother, the Sindhu, is far away from them. But wherever they are in the world, they remember the sacred river and the great *avatara* who arose from the river to protect them:

"Jeko Chavando Jhoolelal,
Tahinja Theenda Beda Paar!
Bolo Jhoolelal, Beda Paar!"

Whoso utters the name of Jhoolelal - all his works will be fulfilled.